D1234886

MEDIEVAL AND MODERN GREEK

Modern Languages

Editor

R. AUTY
M.A., Dr. Phil.
Professor of Comparative Slavonic Philology
in the University of Oxford

MEDIEVAL AND
MODERN GREEK

Robert Browning
Professor of Classics and Ancient History
Birkbeck College, University of London

HUTCHINSON UNIVERSITY LIBRARY
LONDON

HUTCHINSON & CO (*Publishers*) LTD
178–202 Great Portland Street, London W1

London Melbourne Sydney
Auckland Bombay Toronto
Johannesburg New York

First published 1969

*The love poem in vernacular Greek on the cover
of the paperback edition is reproduced from a
fifteenth-century MS by courtesy of the Trustees
of the British Museum*

*This book has been set in Times New Roman, printed in
Great Britain on Smooth Wove paper by William Clowes
and Sons, Limited, London and Beccles, and bound by
Wm. Brendon, Tiptree, Essex*

09 099600 3 (cased)
09 099601 1 (paper)

For

TAMARA AND ANNA

CONTENTS

PREFACE

The Homeric poems were first written down in more or less their present form in the seventh century B.C. Since then Greek has enjoyed a continuous tradition down to the present day. Change there has certainly been. But there has been no break like that between Latin and the Romance languages. Ancient Greek is not a foreign language to the Greek of today, as Anglo-Saxon is to the modern Englishman. The only other language which enjoys comparable continuity of tradition is Chinese.

The study of Greek in England, as in most other countries, has traditionally been concentrated upon the classical language. The New Testament was left to theologians, and a nineteenth-century schoolboy who attempted to imitate it in his prose composition would have got short shrift from his teacher. The medieval and modern stages of the language were largely ignored.

Today the situation has changed. There is a widespread interest in Modern Greek. And the Byzantine world attracts the attention of students of history, literature and art. Classical scholars no longer regard it as beneath their dignity to concern themselves with the Greek of the middle ages and modern times.

The present volume aims to provide an introduction to the development of the Greek language from the Hellenistic age to the present day. It will be of use primarily to those who know some ancient Greek and who wish to explore the later history of the language. But it is the author's hope that it will also be helpful to those who have learnt Modern Greek and who seek some guidance in their approach to the medieval or classical language. It cannot be too much emphasised that Greek is one language, and not a series of distinct languages. If one wants to learn Greek, it does not really matter whether one begins with Homer, with Plato, with the New Testament, with the Romance of Digenis Akritas, or with Kazantzakis. The effort required to tackle earlier or later stages, once the student is firmly grounded in one stage, is not great. And educated Greek speakers have always had present in their minds the whole of the language up to their own time, drawn upon it, alluded to it, and consciously modified it. It is this intellectual continuity which makes the study of Greek both rewarding and difficult.

Thanks are due to Miss Susan Archer, who typed the awkward manuscript, most of it several times; to Mrs Patsy Vanags, who read the proofs; to Miss Ann Douglas of Messrs Hutchinson for her painstaking and skilled help in seeing the book through the press: and to my many Greek students for supplying information, often without knowing they were doing it.

July 1969   ROBERT BROWNING

I

INTRODUCTORY

Speakers of Greek entered the southern part of the Balkan peninsula in the first half of the second millennium B.C.[1] From then until the present day they have formed the overwhelming majority of the population of the region. From this nucleus Greek spread to become the language of both isolated settlements and large areas all round the Mediterranean coast as well as of the greater part of the land mass of Asia Minor.[2] In addition it served at various times as a language of culture, of administration, of trade in areas where it was not the native language of the mass of the population: it fulfilled this role as far east as the foothills of the Pamir and the Indus valley in Hellenistic times,[3] throughout Egypt and beyond its frontiers to the south in Hellenistic and Roman times, in the Slavonic-speaking areas of the northern Balkan peninsula during the middle ages. Lastly there have existed at various periods, including the present, compact communities of Greek speakers settled in areas of non-Greek speech, and often maintaining their identity and their national consciousness for many generations; examples which spring to the mind are the Greek trading community of Southern Gaul of which St Ignatius was a member, the 'hungry Greeklings' of Juvenal's Rome – one of whom was St Clement, the Greek village of Cargèse in Corsica,[4] the Greek communities of the present-day United States,[5] the Greek communities of Odessa and Alexandria, the Hellenophone Cypriot community of London.[6]

In spite of its geographical extension and the existence of

[1] Superior figures refer to bibliographical notes at the end of the chapters.

Greek-speaking enclaves far from the main mass of speakers of the language, Greek has always remained one language. There have been in the past and are today considerable dialectal differences. But neither in the past nor today have they been sufficiently great to impede communication between speakers of different dialects. Nor has there ever been in historic times any other language even partially intelligible to Greek speakers without special study.[7] No Greek speaker was or is ever in doubt whether another man's speech is Greek or not. Though local dialects have sometimes acquired prestige as vehicles of literature outside the area in which they were spoken, there has never been any tendency for Greek to break up into a series of languages either mutually not fully intelligible or felt by their speakers to be distinct, as Vulgar Latin broke up into the various Romance languages.

Perhaps connected with this continuous identity over some three and a half millennia is the slowness of change in Greek. It is still recognisably the same language today as it was when the Homeric poems were written down, probably around 700 B.C., though it must be observed that the traditional orthography masks many of the phonological changes which have taken place.[8] The continuity of lexical stock is striking – though here too things are not as simple as they seem at first sight. And though there has been much rearrangement of morphological patterns, there has also been much continuity, and Greek is quite clearly even today an archaic, 'Indo-European' type of language, like Latin or Russian, not a modern, analytical language, like English or Persian. Earlier stages of the language are thus accessible to speakers of later stages, in a way that Anglo-Saxon or even middle English is not accessible to speakers of modern English.

Greek was first written in a syllabary adapted from one designed for a non-Hellenic, and probably non-Indo-European, language in the second half of the second millennium B.C.[9] However, with the collapse of the Mycenean civilisation this syllabary seems to have been quickly forgotten, and Greece reverted to illiteracy for several centuries. It is uncertain when or by whom the Phoenician alphabet was adapted to represent Greek by using certain superfluous consonant signs to indicate vowels. But by the late eighth century B.C. several varieties of the new Greek alphabet were in use for sepulchral and other inscriptions.[10] From this early period date also a number of casual verses and personal remarks scratched on pottery or carved on natural rock surface, which

bear witness to the use of the new alphabetic writing for 'un-
official' purposes and to widespread familiarity with it. Perhaps
the earliest Greek 'literary' text is a line and a half of verse containing an allusion to the cup of Nestor described in the Iliad,
which is scratched on a jug recently found in Ischia, and plausibly
dated to the third quarter of the eighth century.[11] By the sixth
century at the latest the study of reading and writing was being
added to the traditional curriculum of gymnastics and music in
some cities. From that date until the present day there has been
a continuous and uninterrupted literary tradition, maintained by
schools, by a body of grammatical literature, by the continuous
study of a limited number of literary texts, whose linguistic form
came to differ more and more from that of current speech. The
prestige of these literary texts was high, and they came more and
more to serve as models for formal speech and writing. By the
first century of our era a new kind of diglossy had begun – new
in the sense that it was something more than the usual opposition
between dialect and standard language, between casual and more
formal utterance, between prose and poetry, and so on. The
reasons for this development will be discussed later. What we
are here concerned with is the continuous pressure exercised
through schools and other institutionalised means in favour of
language patterns which enjoyed prestige, and in particular of
archaic patterns, and the corresponding discrimination against
those features of living speech which were felt to clash with the
prescribed patterns. The effect of this pressure on the development of the spoken language was probably extremely slight until
recently; literacy was never, in ancient times or in the middle
ages, sufficiently widespread. But it did mean that any formal
utterance, and in particular any written sample of language,
differed considerably from 'normal' speech. The degree of difference varied. Imitation of all the features of the models was an
unattainable goal, even for those who devoted the main effort
of their lives to it. All literature and all written documents of
late antiquity and the middle ages show a mixture of diverse
elements, the continuously developing language of the people
being adulterated in varying degrees and in various ways by
classicising Greek. This is true even of texts ostensibly written
in popular Greek. The knowledge of writing put its possessor
in touch with the classicising tradition, and writing could not be
practised without making concessions to that tradition.

Thus in spite of the large number of texts surviving from all

periods, it is often extremely difficult to trace the development
of the language as actually used in most situations. The real process of change is masked by a factitious, classicising uniformity.
For the period up to the eleventh century A.D. we are dependent
largely on negative evidence, i.e. on what the grammarians enjoin their pupils not to do. This evidence can be supplemented
for the earlier part of the period – up to the middle of the seventh
century – by that of non-literary papyri from Egypt, containing
letters, shopping lists, tax receipts, petitions, and the like. But
it must be borne in mind that the writers of these are usually
trying their best – which may be not a very good best – to write
purist Greek; their evidence is never unequivocal. A further check
is provided by a series of literary texts which make concessions
to the spoken language. These are mainly world chronicles, tales
of ascetics, and lives of saints. Examples are the *Chronicle* of
John Malalas (sixth century) and the *Chronography* of Theophanes (early ninth century), *The Spiritual Meadow* of John
Moschos (*c.* 600), the lives of Palestinian saints by Cyril of Scy-
thopolis (sixth century) and the *Life of St John the Almsgiver* by
Leontios of Neapolis in Cyprus (seventh century). None of these
works is in any sense a reproduction of contemporary spoken
Greek; they are mixtures of living speech and dead tradition,
like all medieval Greek texts. One must in each case try to determine the proportions of the mixture, and also the reason for the
adoption of this particular literary form: it may be important
to know whether we are dealing with an incompetent attempt to
write purist Greek or with the work of a man of learning who
tries to make concessions to uneducated readers or hearers. A
further practical difficulty is the scarcity of lexica, indexes and
grammatical studies of early medieval Greek texts, whether purist
or sub-standard.[12] We often do not know what is 'normal', however we may define that term.

In the later medieval and early modern periods we have a great
deal more direct evidence. There is a large body of literature,
mostly poetry, written in a linguistic form which is clearly not
that of contemporary purist literature.[13] To take only a few
examples, there are the vernacular prodromic poems of the
middle of the twelfth century, the poems of Michael Glykas of
the same period, the *Chronicle of the Morea* from the end of the
thirteenth century, a group of verse romances which are difficult
to date exactly, but which probably belong to the thirteenth or
fourteenth century, the epic poems on Achilles and Belisarios,

various popular treatments of the theme of the Trojan War, laments on the fall of Constantinople, the poem on the plague at Rhodes of Emmanuel Georgillas (end of the fifteenth century), the poems of the Cretans Georgios Choumnos, Stephanos Sachlikes and Marinos Phalieros (same period), a group of love poems in Cypriot dialect, probably of the sixteenth century, and the extensive and important literature of the Cretan school of the later sixteenth and seventeenth centuries, culminating in the *Erotokritos* of Vintsentzos Kornaros.

Here we seem to be treading firmer ground. No single line of any of these poems could possibly be supposed to be intended as purist Greek. And certain of them are written in a dialect whose forms are often remote from those of the literary language. But appearances may be deceptive, and close inspection of any of these texts reveals certain disquieting features. For instance, at the lexical level, we find that the Corfiot poet Iakovos Trivolis (first half of the sixteenth century) has three different words for 'lion' in one and the same poem: λέων, λεοντάρι and λιοντάρι. Were these all current in the spoken Greek of his time, or are some of them lexical borrowings from the purist language? At the level of morphology, Trivolis, like many writers of early demotic poetry, uses two forms for the third person plural of the present indicative or subjunctive, -ουσι and -ουν, and two corresponding forms for the third person plural of the imperfect and aorist indicative, -ασι and -αν. Now -ουσι, the Attic and Koine form, is that current in the purist language, while -ουν is that of modern common demotic; and medieval grammarians enjoin the use of -ουσι and warn against that of -ουν. Are the -ουσι forms purist intrusions in the basically demotic language of Trivolis? A further consideration may make us hesitate. Modern Greek dialects are divided between -ουσι and -ουν, -ασι and -αν.[14] Those which use the one do not normally use the other but there are areas where both are in use, e.g. Crete. Have we therefore a mixture of different contemporary dialect forms, such as is often found in a literary language, especially in a nation of travellers like the Greek? We cannot really answer this question without considering the problem of the origin of these terminations. Now -ασι belongs historically to the perfect tense, and -αν to the aorist. In living speech the distinction between the two tenses disappeared in late antiquity, partly thanks to the coincidence of certain perfect and aorist forms, but mainly owing to the restructuring of the system of aspects in early medieval Greek.[15]

In medieval purist Greek the two tenses are formally distinguished, but are semantically equivalent. Are the -ασι forms due to the influence of the purist language? Do they owe their preservation to the analogy of the -ουσι forms of the present? Was there really a choice in sixteenth-century spoken Greek between -ουσι and -ουν, -ασι and -αν, a choice which was resolved in later common demotic in favour of -ουν and -αν? These are questions which it would be premature to seek to answer at this stage, and to which an answer is sometimes impossible in the present state of our knowledge. But they are questions which are squarely posed by lines in which both forms are found side by side, such as τόσον ἐκεῖνοι ποὺ ποθοῦν, ὅσα ποὺ δὲν ποθοῦσι 'as much those who desire it as those who do not desire it',[16] and by parallel formulae in which now the one form, now the other occurs, like φωνάζασι μεγάλα 'cry aloud' and 'καστὶ καοὺρ' φωνάζαν 'cry "Kasti giaour"'.[17]

Similarly, Trivolis uses both the modern demotic nominative form ὁ πατέρας 'the father' and the purist genitive singular form τοῦ πατρός. Were both patterns of declension familiar in the spoken Greek of his time, or is the latter a classicising reminiscence? The existence of gen. sings. in -ός, e.g. τῆς ἡμερός 'of the day', in certain dialects may be relevant. When we find the author of the *Chronicle of the Morea* regularly using the purist nominative singular form θυγάτηρ 'daughter' (the demotic form is θυγατέρα) not only as a nominative, but also as an accusative, e.g. v.2492: καὶ χαιρετᾷ τοῦ βασιλέως ἐκείνου τὴν θυγάτηρ 'and greets the daughter of that King', we are clearly dealing with an ill-conceived attempt at literary style by a writer who is in general relatively immune to the influence of the purist tradition; the poem was probably composed by a Hellenised Frank and a Catholic, and it is in fact uncertain whether the Greek or the Old French version is the original. The analogical argument underlying this bastard form, which is neither purist Greek nor demotic is as follows: the demotic form θυγατέρα functions both as nominative and accusative, as is normal for feminine substantives; to θυγατέρα in its nominative function the corresponding purist form is θυγάτηρ; this is then extended in scope to correspond to demotic θυγατέρα in its accusative function; the true purist accusative form is actually θυγατέρα, which is felt to be demotic and thus insufficiently elevated for the description of a royal personage. Thus we see that even a poet as remote from the Byzantine literary tradition as the author of the *Chronicle of the Morea* is affected by it, perhaps unconsciously, as soon as he takes his pen in his hand, or dictates something to be read aloud.

At the level of syntax we find in Trivolis both infinitives and subjunctive clauses introduced by νά after θέλω in the periphrastic future, e.g. εἰπεῖν ἤθελα, κάμειν ἤθελα, θέλετε τὴν ἀκούσει, θέλει ἐλθεῖ, θὲς εὑρεῖ, θὲς ἰδεῖ, ἤθελα ἐμπῆ side by side with θὲς νὰ μετατρέψης, θὲ νὰ κρεμάσω. Now the infinitive had long vanished from demotic Greek in most of its usages long before the sixteenth century. It is therefore tempting to dismiss Trivolis' infinitives as learned forms, alien to the spoken Greek of his time. But it is noteworthy that he does not use infinitive forms except after θέλω. Future forms in medieval Greek are peculiarly labile. The ancient Greek future forms were already ceasing to be distinctive in the Koine as a result of phonological changes, and a variety of periphrases with ἔχω, θέλω etc. are found in the less purist texts of late antiquity and the middle ages.[18] It cannot be ruled out that θέλω plus infinitive was a living form in the spoken Greek of the sixteenth century, side by side with the alternative pattern θέλω νά plus subjunctive, which is the ancestor of the modern demotic future form θά plus subjunctive.[19] A slightly different problem is exemplified by the construction of the indirect object. Dative forms had long vanished from living use, except in isolated phrases surviving as lexical items by the late middle ages.[20] In many of the poems under discussion we find side by side two patterns, accusative of indirect object and genitive of indirect object, e.g. *Chronicle of the Morea* v. 2486: σπουδαίως μαντάτα τοῦ ἤφεραν ἐκεῖσε εἰς τὸ κάστρον 'swiftly they brought him orders thither to the castle' and ibid. v. 2500: λέγουσιν τὸν μισὶρ Τζεφρὲ καὶ συμβουλεύσουσίν τον 'they speak to Monsieur Geoffroi and counsel him'. Now in modern Greek the dialects are divided sharply on this point. The dialects of Macedonia, Thrace and Thessaly have σὲ δίνω, those of the rest of Greece σοῦ δίνω in the sense of 'I give you'.[21] In no dialect are both patterns habitually found. Modern common demotic, being based on southern dialects, has σοῦ δίνω. We know very little of the regional dialects of spoken Greek in the thirteenth century. It may be that the Peloponnesian vernacular familiar to the author of the Chronicle permitted both patterns. Or it may be that he is adulterating his native speech with a syntactical pattern from another dialect, which for some reason seemed to him more suitable for elevated utterance.[22]

Examples of this kind, at every level of linguistic analysis,

could be multiplied indefinitely from the non-purist literature of
the middle ages and later. All this literature is written in a mixture of developing spoken Greek and static purist Greek.[23] The
proportions of the mixture vary both between different texts and
between different linguistic levels. But nowhere do we have a
specimen of the spoken language of the time. In the past some
scholars have failed to take account of this, and have supposed
that each text was in principle written in a formalised version of
the spoken language of the writer, and that therefore these texts
offered direct evidence for the development of the spoken language. Jean Psichari (1854–1929) the leading champion of the
literary use of demotic at the end of the nineteenth century, and
a Hellenist of impressive range and infectious enthusiasm, wasted
many years in the compilation of statistics of the use of various
morphological features, in the mistaken impression that he was
tracing the development of vernacular Greek. He thus succeeded
in dating most developments much too late, and in postulating
their occurrence in an order which makes no sense.[24] His great
contemporary and rival, Georgios Chatzidakis (1849–1941),
pointed out that the proportion of old to new forms depends
largely on the degree of education of the writer, and that statistics
of the kind amassed by Psichari were of no value for the chrono-
logy of the development of the language.[25] He emphasised that
what was important was to date the earliest occurrence of a new
feature in the texts; this was what enabled us to reconstruct the
history of the living, spoken language. Chatzidakis was right in
principle. But, like most scholars of his generation, brought up
under the influence of the German Neo-Grammarians (Jung-
grammatiker), he overlooked two points of some importance.
The first is that one linguistic feature does not simply replace
another at a given moment of time. Both the old and the new may
coexist in living speech, indeed must for some time. Where there
is a long and continuous literary tradition, where therefore the
archaic enjoys prestige, and earlier states of the language are
maintained in the consciousness of its speakers, one would expect
this coexistence of the old and the new to be particularly marked.
In the case of Greek we must bear in mind not only the direct
influence of the purist language upon the literate, but its indirect
influence upon the illiterate, who hear it used on occasions of
solemnity or by persons enjoying prestige in society: the familiarity of the vast majority of Greeks with the language of the
Orthodox liturgy is particularly important in this connection.[26]

It is therefore *a priori* probable that at any given time a speaker of Greek had before him a larger choice of linguistic patterns than a speaker of a language with no recorded literature and no traditional system of education. It is important to try to distinguish between alternatives within the spoken language and borrowings from purist Greek. Frequency counts, conducted with due precautions, may be of use for this purpose. To this extent Psichari was working on the right lines.

The second point in regard to which the work of the generation of Psichari and Chatzidakis is seen today to be inadequate is their tendency to regard linguistic changes as atomic. This inflection is replaced by that, two phonemes coincide, this or that tense or case falls out of use, as if each individual change was independent of all others. What they and their generation did not take into account is that language, at all its levels, is structured, and that phonological, morphological and syntactic changes, and to a lesser extent lexical changes, are generally only individual manifestations of a change in the structural pattern of the language at some level.[27] Thus when we find indications that -ες was replacing -αι in the nominative plural of first declension nouns, or that perfect and aorist forms of the verb were being used as equivalents, these are only symptoms of the reorganisation of the nominal declension in such a way as to efface the old distinction between vocalic and consonantal stems, on the one hand, and the reorganisation of the system of tenses and aspects of the verb on the other. In the succeeding chapters attention will be concentrated on the large structural changes rather than on the detailed changes of morphology and syntax. To some extent this method of approach enables us to surmount the difficulty alluded to in the previous paragraph of distinguishing between incidental imitations of purist Greek and real alternatives coexisting in the spoken tongue. Care must be taken, however, not to involve ourselves in circular arguments in this connection. And we must bear in mind that different structural patterns can coexist in the spoken language as alternatives.

The foregoing considerations give some idea of the precautions necessary in using the evidence of medieval texts to reconstruct the history of the spoken language, which stem largely from the continuity of the literary tradition and the accompanying diglossy. This diglossy is not a simple matter of the coexistence of a literary and a spoken version of the same language, but of the presence of an abnormally wide choice of alternative modes of expression in the spoken language, plus a varying degree of admixture of lexical, syntactical and morphological elements belonging to, or thought by writers or speakers to belong to, an archaising and relatively unchanging purist language.

Periodisation of the history of the spoken language is therefore difficult, and inevitably only approximate.[28] It is clear, however, that behind the curtain of traditional linguistic uniformity, the modern Greek language had largely assumed its form by the tenth century. In the following chapters particular attention will be concentrated on the period between the late Hellenistic Koine of the Roman empire and the tenth century. From the tenth to the fifteenth century we have, it is true, a great number of texts which show strong vernacular characteristics. These serve to illustrate the changes which can sometimes be only faintly traced in the foregoing centuries. Certain developments, in particular the tidying up of the structure of nominal declension, and the adoption of extensive lexical loans from other languages, can confidently be placed in this period. The third period, from the fifteenth century to 1821, is one in which, for all the relative abundance of material, it is not easy to detect developments in the spoken tongue. To it belong the formation of a more or less standardised Cretan literary dialect, its replacement by an incipient literary language in the Ionian Islands, and the first steps toward the creation of modern standard demotic. The fourth period, from 1821 to the present day, is marked by the emergence of the 'Language Question', when the traditional diglossy begins to present peculiar problems to those bent on forging a modern national language and an educational system based upon it, and acquires political overtones which it did not possess in the earlier period. For it must be borne in mind that while Greek diglossy extends over two millennia, the language question arises only with the birth of the Greek state. Other features of the fourth period are the rejection of a large number of Turkish loan-words which had become current in the language in the preceding period, and the immense lexical enrichment of the language as it became a vehicle of modern scientific, philosophical, political and literary expression.

This enrichment took place in part by the adoption of loan-words from other European languages, at first French and later English. But the existence of a continuous literary tradition enabled the language to augment its lexical stock largely from Greek sources, by the revival of obsolete words, the semantic modifications of existing words, the formation of linguistic calques, and above all by a complex process of internal borrowing between the traditional purist language and the developing demotic. These processes will be dealt with in detail in subsequent chapters, but a brief survey of the vocabulary elements of modern demotic will throw further light on what is the main theme of this introductory chapter – the peculiar situation created by a long and continuous literary tradition which makes all elements of Greek from antiquity to the present day in a sense accessible and 'present' to any literate Greek.

First there are words continuous in form and in meaning since classical times, e.g. ἀδελφός 'brother' (though most dialects, and often common demotic, prefer ἀδερφός in accordance with a regular phonetic development), γράφω 'write', ἄλλος 'other'. Then there are words modified in form in accordance with phonological and morphological developments, but identical in meaning with their classical Greek ancestors, e.g. μέρα 'day', βρίσκω 'find', ψηλός 'high', to which the corresponding classical Greek forms are ἡμέρα, εὑρίσκω, ὑψηλός. Next come words continuous in form since classical times, but whose meaning has changed, e.g. μετάνοια 'genuflection', χῶμα 'soil', στοιχίζω 'cost', φθάνω 'arrive'. Corresponding to these is a series of words which have undergone normal phonological or morphological development, and also a change of meaning, e.g. ντρέπομαι 'am ashamed', περιβόλι 'garden', ἀκριβός 'dear'.[29] Alongside of these four groups are four corresponding groups of words descended from neologisms of post-classical Koine Greek. First, those continuous in form and meaning, e.g. κατόρθωμα 'success', ἐπιστημονικός 'scientific', φωτίζω 'illuminate'. Next, those modified in form but identical in meaning, e.g. μοιάζω 'resemble', συζήτηση 'discussion', ὁλόγυρα 'around'. Third, those continuous in form but modified in meaning, e.g. παραμονή 'vigil before a feast', λάθος 'mistake', σοβαρός 'serious', περιορίζω 'define'. And lastly, those modified both in form and in meaning, e.g. ἄνοιξη 'spring', σηκώνω 'lift up', ψωμί 'bread'.

The next major segment of the vocabulary consists of medieval or early modern neologisms formed from earlier existing roots or stems by derivation or composition, e.g. πέρνω 'take', μαζεύω 'gather', κορίτσι 'girl', χαμόγελο 'smile', βαρυσήμαντος 'important', ἀργά 'slowly'.

A further segment consists of classical or Hellenistic words reintroduced to the spoken tongue via the purist katharevousa, either with unchanged or with slightly modified meaning, but almost certainly not in continuous use throughout the middle ages, e.g. διάστημα 'space', πρόεδρος 'chairman', αὐτοκίνητο 'automobile', ἀερίζω 'ventilate', ἐντύπωση 'impression'.

Needless to say, these may be modified where necessary in accordance with demotic phonology and morphology. But in this respect the situation is by no means simple, as will become clear in the discussion of the relation between the different states of the language today.

The next segment, and it is a very large and 'open-ended' one – consists of new words formed in Modern Greek by derivation or composition from classical or Koine Greek elements. Some of these appear to have arisen in the first place in the spoken language, others in the katharevousa. They readily pass from katharevousa to demotic, and occasionally in the opposite direction, usually with the necessary adjustments of form. Examples are γραφεῖον 'office', ἐξαιρετικός 'exceptional', ἐνδιαφέρον 'interest', γλωσσο-λόγος 'linguist', πεζοδρόμιο 'pavement', πανεπιστήμιο 'university', ἐκτόξευσις 'blast-off'.[30]

Akin to these entirely Greek formations, and once they have become current, not distinguished from them by native speakers, is the segment consisting of international words, formed in western Europe from Greek elements, and adopted, with the necessary morphological adjustments, into Greek, e.g. ἀτμό-σφαιρα 'atmosphere', μηχανισμός 'mechanism', φωτογραφία 'photography', κοσμοναύτης 'cosmonaut'.

Side by side with these there is a large segment of words formed in modern Greek from Greek elements as calques of foreign words or expressions; the model is most usually French. Examples are ὑπερφυσικός 'super-natural', ἐθνικιστής 'nationalist', ἐκτελεστικός 'executive', ἀκαλαισθησία 'bad taste', νευρικότητα 'nervousness', πραγματοποιῶ 'realise', σκηνοθεσία 'mise en scene', ψυχραιμία 'sang-froid', προσωπικό 'personnel', διαστημόπλοιο 'space-ship'. There is no clear line to be drawn between this seg-ment of the vocabulary and that discussed two paragraphs earlier. French, and to a lesser extent English, were widely known in educated circles in Greece in the nineteenth and twentieth cen-turies, and they inevitably served as models in the sense that they suggested what vocabulary elements were missing in Greek. But there is clearly a difference in the degree of correspondence between foreign model and Greek equivalent between, say, ἐκτόξευσις and διαστημόπλοιο, which enables us to classify the former as an independent creation from Greek elements and the latter as a mechanical calque of the English 'spaceship'.

The next category is that of loan-words from foreign languages which have been adapted to Greek phonological and morphological requirements. Many of these are felt by native speakers to be Greek words, and all can readily be used without conflicting with the structural patterns of the language. Lexical borrowing has been going on in Greek for a very long time; indeed the linear B texts of the second millennium B.C. and the Homeric poems contain many loan-words from pre-Hellenic languages. But we are here concerned with loan-words in post-classical Greek. The earliest stratum is that of Latin loan-words, such as σπίτι 'house', πόρτα 'door', κουβεντιάζω 'converse'. The next large segment consists of Italian loan-words, which may in their turn be classified according to the dialect from which they were borrowed. Examples are γκρίζος 'grey', καρέκλα 'chair', μπράτσο 'arm', σιγάρο 'cigarette', φουρτούνα 'storm', φουστάνι 'woman's dress'. There is a considerable segment of Turkish loan-words, such as μενεξές 'violet', καφές 'coffee', ταβατούρι 'disturbance, chaos', τσιμπούκι 'pipe'. But a great many of the Turkish loan-words current in the middle of the nineteenth century have now ceased to be current, and indeed many of them are now quite unknown to Greek speakers. The last main segment of 'assimilated' loan-words is that from French, Italian and English, usually of quite recent date, e.g. ἀρριβίστας 'arriviste', πορτραῖτο 'portrait', προλετάριος 'proletarian', τορπιλλίζω 'torpedo'. In addition to these large segments of loan-words, there are smaller numbers from Iranian in the middle ages, from South Slavonic, e.g. ντόμπρος 'kind', or Albanian, e.g. λουλούδι 'flower', in the later middle ages or in early modern times, and from Russian and other languages in the most recent period.

Among the loan-words of modern demotic we must count also those classical or Koine words and expressions preserved in the purist katharevousa, and borrowed thence into demotic. They usually retain their katharevousa phonology and morphology. Examples are ἀμείλικτος 'implacable', λευκός 'white', οἶκος 'house',[31] συγκεχειμένος 'confused', ἀδιαφορῶ 'am indifferent', συνεχῶς 'continuously', πράγματι 'in fact', τουναντίον 'on the contrary'. Many writers of demotic, and certain rather pompous speakers of it, extend this category of loan-words by using classical or Koine words preserved in katharevousa, even when there is a perfectly good demotic synonym available.

There is another class of loan-word, which is not adapted to modern Greek phonological or morphological patterns, either katharevousa or demotic. These words tend to enjoy rather a short vogue, and then either to pass out of use or to be fitted into Greek patterns. Examples are παστέλ 'pastel', τζάζ 'jazz', μπάρ 'bar', χιουμόρ 'humour', σπόρ 'sport', νίκελ 'nickel'. As an example of the mode of adaptation of these loan-words, it is interesting to note that derivatives, of morphologically regular pattern, are often formed, e.g. from νίκελ we have νικέλινος 'nickel' adj., νικελώνω 'to nickel-plate', νικέλωμα 'nickel-plate', νικέλωση 'process of nickel-plating', and that the form νικέλιο is now found side by side with the unassimilated νίκελ.

The last segment of the vocabulary consists of dialect words used for special effect. Certain writers, such as Kazantzakis, make very extensive use of these internal borrowings, some of which thereby become permanent elements of the vocabulary of common demotic.

This analysis of the sources of the vocabulary applies in particular to modern common demotic Greek. But a similar analysis of the vocabulary of the living language at other periods would reveal a similar complexity, even if all the categories of present-day Greek were not present. The vocabulary of Greek at all periods is extremely rich, and this richness depends in part on the possibility of using elements belonging to earlier states of the language, which always remain accessible, and which may have special emotional overtones attached to them.[32] There is also a good deal of polysemy, in that the same word may be used with several different meanings, which originally belonged to it in different states of the language. Only the context, both linguistic and extra-linguistic, determines the particular meaning. For instance, σκαλλίζω means not only 'sculpt, engrave', but also preserves its earlier meanings 'dig up' and 'investigate', the last depending on a metaphorical use in the Septuagint version of Psalm 76.6; σύνταξη, in addition to its inherited meanings of 'arrangement' and 'syntax', also means 'pension'; ἀπαντῶ, of which the classical and Koine meaning is 'meet', and the commonest meaning in demotic 'answer', is listed in the 'Ιστορικὸν Λεξικὸν τῆς Νεοελληνικῆς with nine current demotic meanings. It is no doubt this polysemy and its attendant vagueness of meaning which underlies the very frequent use of pairs of synonyms linked by καί in medieval and early modern literature.

1. Starr (1962) 30–36; Caskey (1965); Chadwick (1963); Vermeule (1964) give a balanced survey of the archaeological picture. It is still extremely difficult to connect archaeological and linguistic evidence.

2. Boardman (1964) for the earlier period. There is no good book on the Hellenisation of Asia Minor.

3. Tarn (1938); Narain (1957); Woodcock (1966).

4. Blanken (1947), (1951).

5. Seaman (1965).

6. George and Millerson (1966/7).

7. Macedonian was probably closely related to Greek, and may have been partially intelligible to Greeks. But Alexander the Great's use of Macedonian in a tight corner suggests that it was not understood by the run of Greeks (Plutarch, *Alex.* 51.4). The Molossi and various other tribal communities of Epirus in ancient times may also have spoken languages akin to Greek, but we know nothing about them.

8. Failure to recognise the irrelevance of an orthography which was no longer phonological has often led to the postulation of ghost-words or ghost-forms. cf. Palmer (1934), (1939), (1945) 1–5.

9. Chadwick (1958) gives a popular but authoritative account. The now immense literature of the subject can best be followed through the annual bibliography and index, *Studies in Mycenean Inscriptions and Dialect*, published by the Institute of Classical Studies of the University of London, 1956 ff.

10. Jeffery (1961); Lejeune (1966); Diringer (1968).

11. Buchner and Russo (1955).

12. Psaltes (1913) offers a very useful collection of material. There are no lexica or concordances to any of these authors. Recent important studies in which references to the earlier literature will be found, include Mihevc-Gabrovec (1960); Weierholt (1963); Tabachovitz (1943); Linnér (1943); Wolff (1961); Zilliacus (1967).

13. For a survey of this early demotic literature and its problems cf. Knös (1962). Knös does not touch on linguistic problems.

14. -ουσι and -ασι are found in Cyprus, Crete, certain of the Sporades and in South Italy, i.e. in a peripheral belt. cf. Thumb (1895) § 165.

15. Mihevc (1959).

16. Irmscher (1956) 64.

17. ibid. 44, 46 (N.B. anomalous accentuation of φωνάζαν, perhaps on the analogy of φωνάζασι).

18. Bănescu (1915); Pernot (1946).

19. The chronicles and early demotic texts, such as Spaneas, Glykas, Ptochoprodromus have only a few uncertain cases of $θέλω$ + inf. as a future periphrasis. It becomes much commoner in the later demotic poetry and is accompanied by a variety of alternative forms; cf. Pernot (1946).

20. Humbert (1930).

21. Triantaphyllides (1938) 66, 81.

22. On this problem, which arises in connection with many medieval Greek texts, cf. Pernot (1946) 158.

23. Böhlig (1957).

24. This is an oversimplified statement of Psichari's views. For a more detailed and nuanced appreciation cf. Mirambel (1957). Nevertheless it remains true that most of the material so laboriously collected in Psichari (1886–1889) is irrelevant to the problems which the author was trying to solve.

25. Chatzidakis' position was maintained in a number of major works, of which the most important are Chatzidakis (1892), (1905) and (1915).

26. Antoniadis (1939).

27. Greek scholars have on the whole shown little interest in structural linguistics. The most important work by structuralists in the field of post-classical and modern Greek has been done by André Mirambel – e.g. Mirambel (1959), and a long series of articles in the *Bulletin de la Société de Linguistique* and elsewhere, Hans-Jakob Seiler – Seiler (1952), (1958) etc., and other scholars working outside of Greece.

28. Kapsomenos (1958) 2; Mirambel (1963); Chatzidakis (1930).

29. ἀκριβής, the classical form preserved in the purist language and borrowed thence by demotic, means 'accurate', hence the adverbs ἀκριβά 'dear' and ἀκριβῶς 'accurately'.

30. Being a word coined by journalists, it generally appears in its purist form ἐκτόξευσις, but the demotic form ἐκτόξευση is met with. On this point see the later discussion on pp. 113.

31. N.B. ὁ Λευκὸς Οἶκος is the White House in Washington, ἄσπρο σπίτι is any white house.

32. The most recent general studies of the vocabulary of modern Greek are Mirambel (1959) 337–450, and van Dijk-Wittop Koning (1963).

2

GREEK IN THE HELLENISTIC WORLD AND

THE ROMAN EMPIRE

The starting-point for any history of medieval and modern Greek must be the κοινὴ διάλεκτος or common Greek of the Hellenistic world. This form of the language was from the first the vehicle of communication at all levels in the new Greek cities which were founded between the Aegean coast of Asia Minor and the plains of the Punjab, from the Syr-Darya in the North to the island of Sokotra in the South. In old Greece it rapidly became the official language of administration and more slowly ousted the old dialects as a general means of communication. At the same time it became the universal language of prose literature, apart from certain highly self-conscious groups which retained a special linguistic form of their own, e.g. the doctors who wrote in the Ionic of the Hippocratic corpus, and the Pythagorean philosophers who wrote in the Doric of Southern Italy. Poetry continued to be written in the traditional linguistic forms, though these were more and more affected by the κοινὴ διάλεκτος.[1]

The origin of the κοινὴ διάλεκτος is really irrelevant to the history of later Greek. In the past it was the subject of much discussion. Today many of the points earlier in dispute are now clear. I shall confine myself to reproducing the generally accepted view on the origin of the Koine, and then go on to describe it, emphasising in particular the changes which can be detected in the course of its development.

In the areas which had long been of Greek speech there was

in the fourth century B.C. no linguistic unity. Each city state used
for official business its own dialect, which was also the normal
means of intercourse between its citizens. The dialects were
mutually comprehensible without difficulty, and most Greeks
must have been used to hearing dialects other than their own
spoken. There was not one but several literary languages – epic
poetry was written in the complex 'Kunstsprache' of the Homeric
tradition, whose roots probably go back to the Mycenean world,
although in its developed form its features were predominantly
Ionic; lyric poetry was written in a Dorising Greek which em-
bodied features not found together in any living dialect; and so
on. The use of these literary languages was determined by the
literary genre, and not by the native dialect of the writer. Prose
literature, which was later in developing than poetry, had been
written in a variety of dialects – in Ionic by most writers of the
early and middle fifth century, in a sort of common Doric by
many writers of Sicily and South Italy, and so on. But by the end
of the fifth century Attic was more and more being used even
by non-Athenians as a vehicle of literary prose. It is typical that
the speeches of Gorgias of Leontini, an Ionian city in eastern
Sicily, which he delivered as models of rhetoric in various cities
of Greece in the closing decades of the fifth century, seem to have
been in Attic.

The political power and intellectual prestige of Athens led to
the increasing use of Attic as a lingua franca of common intercourse in Greece. Athenian officials visited or resided in a great
many cities round the Aegean. Athenian colonists were settled
in a number of points in the region. Citizens of cities subject to
Athens had to an increasing extent to submit their disputes to
the jurisdiction of Athenian courts. At a humbler social level,
many thousands of non-Athenians served as rowers in the
Athenian fleet. The Peiraeus was the great entrepôt of eastern
Mediterranean trade, and both there and in Athens itself a large
community of non-Athenians from all parts of the Greek world
was established. In these and other ways the knowledge and use
of Attic spread in the last third of the fifth century. The military
defeat of Athens in 404 B.C. did not affect the social and economic
pressures which worked in favour of Attic. However, the Attic
thus extensively used outside of Attica was itself modified. Contemporary writers speak of the adoption of words from many
other dialects in the cosmopolitan society of Athens–Peiraeus in
the late fifth century (Ps-Xen. *Ath. Pol.* 2.8). The admixture must

in fact have been mainly Ionic, and have operated at all levels, from phonetics, -σσ- for Attic -ττ-, to vocabulary. At the same time writers, even those of Athenian birth, who counted on a pan-Hellenic readership, themselves avoided some of the more specific features of Attic, and gave their language an Ionic tinge. For instance Thucydides, writing for the whole Greek world, replaces Attic -ττ- by Ionic (and to some extent common Hellenic) -σσ-, -ρρ- by -ρσ- and so on, while the Old Oligarch (the author of the polemical treatise on the Constitution of Athens erroneously attributed by the manuscript tradition to Xenophon), writing a political pamphlet for Athenian readers, uses the Attic forms. These two factors, working at different levels, resulted in the 'expanded Attic' which was the common language of much of Greece in the fourth century, being significantly different from the pure dialect spoken by Attic peasants.

In the fourth century, Attic, whether in its pure or its 'expanded' form was the normal language of literary prose. Not only Athenians like Xenophon, Isocrates, Demosthenes and Plato wrote in Attic, but men from other parts of Greece, whose native dialects differed both from Attic and from one another: Aeneas of Stymphalos, Aristotle of Stageira, Deinarchus of Corinth, Theophrastus of Eresos in Lesbos, Ephoros of Kyme in Asia Minor, Theopompos of Chios, Anaximenes of Lampsakos, and others.

Thus, when in the middle of the fourth century Philip II of Macedonia determined to elevate his backward tribal kingdom to the status of a great power, he adopted Attic as the official language of Macedonian diplomacy and administration. His son Alexander carried Macedonian power as far as Egypt, the Pamirs and the river Jumna. Attic, in its 'expanded' international form became the official language and the language of everyday intercourse of the multitude of Greek cities founded in the conquered territories by Alexander and his successors, cities whose inhabitants usually came from many different regions of Greece. This modified Attic – called by grammarians ἡ κοινὴ διάλεκτος, the common language – thus became the mother tongue of the new Greek communities in Egypt, Syria, Asia Minor, Mesopotamia and the Iranian world, and gradually ousted the old dialects in Greece proper; this point will be examined later. It also became the language of prose literature, with certain minor exceptions, throughout the Greek world. It was a linguistic form which was no longer rooted in the speech of a particular region.

Our knowledge of the Koine depends:

(1) On literary texts composed in it, such as the Histories of Polybius and Diodorus of Sicily, the Discourses of Epictetus.

(2) On the Greek translation of the Hebrew scriptures made in Alexandria in the third century B.C., the Septuagint.

(3) On the New Testament and certain other early Christian writings.

(4) On a mass of letters and other documents surviving on papyrus in Egypt, and dating from the end of the fourth century B.C. to the eighth century A.D.

(5) On the observations of grammarians.[2]

The literary texts show a fairly standardised language, no doubt the medium of formal intercourse among educated men. The Septuagint, being a close translation of a sacred text, embodies many Hebraisms, and is composed in a language much closer to common speech than the literary texts. The New Testament, being written in the main by men without a literary education – and some of its books probably having been originally composed in Aramaic[3] – approximates closely to the language of everyday speech. In the past there was a great deal of discussion of the linguistic form of the N.T. Many scholars believed it to be written in a special variety of Greek in use among the Jewish communities of the Near East and sought in this an explanation of the divergences between its language and that of the literary texts. The evidence provided in the last 75 years by the innumerable letters and documents on papyrus has proved that this is not so, but that the language of the N.T. is a close reflection of the spoken Koine of the Greek world at the time of its composition.[4] Among the literary texts there are several – the Discourses of Epictetus are the prime example – which have many points of contact linguistically with the N.T., being composed in a less carefully standardised form than the bulk of Koine prose literature. The observations of grammarians are mostly by-products of an archaising movement which sought to restore ancient Attic as the language of literature and polite intercourse, a movement of which we shall speak later. The words and forms which they warn their pupils not to use are the Koine words and forms.

The Koine did not remain static, but was in process of continuous development. There were no doubt also local differences within it. The geographer Strabo speaks of local differences of pronunciation within the Greek world. These would probably be most marked in the old areas of Greek settlement, where the old dialects were slow to disappear, and less marked in the vast areas of new settlement, where there was no dialect substratum. But as far as our evidence goes, the Koine was remarkably uniform throughout its area of use. The English of North America rather than that of England, the Spanish of central and South America rather than that of Spain, are appropriate modern parallels. Changes in the language are often difficult to date with precision. The literate tended to maintain in use words and forms which were being replaced in the speech of the mass of the people, and all our evidence comes from the literate. Phonological changes in particular are masked by the historical orthography, and can often only be detected through spelling mistakes in letters and documents on papyrus. In the following paragraphs the main features which distinguished the early Koine from the Attic of classical literature will first be described, and then an account will be given of the principal changes detectable in the course of the centuries between Alexander the Great and Justinian.

PHONOLOGY

The Koine regularly avoids the specifically Attic -ττ- (from guttural plosive +*i̯*), and substitutes the Ionic, and generally pan-Hellenic -σσ-. Thus θάλασσα 'sea', γλῶσσα 'tongue', ὀρύσσω 'dig' not θάλαττα, γλῶττα, ὀρύττω. It is not clear to what phonetic difference this orthographic distinction corresponds. Attic words, for which there is no cognate in Ionic or other dialects, often appear, in Koine with Attic -ττ-, e.g. ἡττάομαι 'am defeated', ἥττημα 'defeat' (N.T. 2 *Pet.* ii, 19, 20, *Rom.* ix, 12, 1 *Cor.* vi, 7) – the Ionic form was ἑσσόομαι (in 2 *Cor.* xii, 13 the reading of the majority of the MSS is ἡσσώθητε, but ancient variants ἡττήθητε and ἐλαττώθητε indicate the uneasiness which copyists felt in the presence of this Ionic but non-Koine form); by analogy ἐλάττων 'lesser' and κρείττων 'greater' sometimes appear in place of the commoner ἐλάσσων and κρείσσων. Similarly, Attic -ρρ- was rejected in favour of Ionic and pan-Hellenic -ρσ-, thus ἄρσην 'male', θάρσος 'courage', not ἄρρην, θάρρος: but πόρρω 'further', because there is no corresponding Ionic form πόρσω. Attic went further than most Greek dialects in contracting two vowels in contact within a word. Koine often prefers to follow the Ionic pattern, thus ἐδέετο 'needed', ἐπλέετο 'sailed' rather than ἐδεῖτο, ἐπλεῖτο.

Thus far the orthography reflects phonological change. But in the early centuries of the Koine a much more important process of phonological change was going on, which is only betrayed by errors in spelling in papyrus documents, Greek loan-words in other languages, foreign loan-words in Greek, and the evidence of spoken Greek today. The vowel system and the consonant system were alike restructured during this period, and the prosodic pattern of the language was reorganised on a new basis. It is difficult to date any of these changes with precision: one can only note the first indication of each which happens to be preserved. In any case what is important is not the individual phonetic change, but the phonological, structural change. And it is likely that for a long period the old and the new patterns existed side by side, either in the same community or even on the lips of the same speaker. Still less can we determine where these changes began. They seem, however, to have spread rapidly over the whole area of Greek speech.

(1) *Vowels*

Attic in the fifth century B.C. had a complex and unstable vowel system, itself in process of change. To the five short vowels a e i o ü there corresponded seven long vowels ā ę̄ ẹ̄ ī ǭ ọ̄ ū. Of the original short diphthongs ai oi üi au eu were still pronounced as true diphthongs; ei and ou had fallen together with ẹ̄ and ọ̄. The long diphthongs āi ę̄i, ǭi, āu ę̄u seem still to have been pronounced as diphthongs. By the end of the second century B.C. this system had been simplified and stabilised. The five short vowels remained unchanged. Of the long vowels ę̄ and ī coincided by the third century (in some dialects, e.g. Boeotian, this change took place earlier; we find confusion of ει and ι in inscriptions of the fifth century), and a century later ẹ̄ and ī began to coincide, though the process seems to have taken a long time to complete. Similarly ǭ became narrowed to ū (a phonetic rather than a phonological change). The diphthongs were restructured too. Original ei and ou had already become monophthongs in classical Attic (ẹ̄ and ọ̄), and ai oi followed them in early Hellenistic becoming e and ü by the second century B.C. In au, eu and the corresponding long diphthongs, the second element became a spirant -av, -ev, -iv. In the long diphthongs āi, ę̄i, ǭi the second element disappeared altogether: Strabo, writing at the end of the first century B.C., remarks that many no longer write the second vowel in these diphthongs, and the evidence of the papyri confirms his observation (Strabo 14.1.41, p. 648). The development of -üi is uncertain: its diphthongal character is often emphasised by spellings such as *vï-*, *vει-*, and attested by grammarians, but this may be due to learned influence. By the fourth century A.D. it had certainly coincided with ü.

At the same time as these changes were taking place, the prosodical pattern of the language was changing. Distinctions of vowel length were ceasing to be phonologically significant, and stress was replacing raised pitch as the distinguishing mark of the accented syllable of a word. This change is not at all easy to detect. But by the end of the third or early second century B.C. confusion between o and ω begins to occur in letters, and a little later we find grammarians giving elaborate rules for the length of vowels – which suggests that their pupils were no longer observing distinctions of length in practice.

The outcome of these changes was to replace the complex vowel system of Attic by a more stable system of six vowels a e i o u ü, with no true diphthongs, which can best be arranged in a triangular pattern:[5]

This is an unusual and not entirely stable system, but it does occur in several languages today.

(2) *Consonants*

At the same time a rearrangement of the consonant system was taking place. Classical Attic – and so far as we can tell other Greek dialects of the same period – had three classes of plosives, unvoiced, voiced, and aspirated: p b p^h, t d t^h, k g k^h, plus the sonants l r m n, the fricative s (z is merely a combinatory variant of s in ancient Greek, as opposed to modern Greek), and the affricate dz; ks and ps are best treated as combinations of phonemes, and are so written in many local varieties of the Greek alphabet. In the Hellenistic period this pattern is changed. Both voiced plosives and aspirated plosives become spirants, voiced and unvoiced respectively. Thus instead of p b p^h we get p v f,

2

instead of t d tʰ, t ð θ, instead of k g kʰ, k ǧ x. In the dental and velar series these changes are hardly attested by the orthography. The evidence consists largely in the transcription of loan-words, and in the state of affairs in modern Greek. In the labial series we have ample evidence in the form of such errors of spelling as κατεσκέβασαν for κατεσκεύασαν 'installed', ῥαῦδος for ῥάβδος 'staff' etc. from the first century B.C. Though any attempt to give a precise date is misleading, it is safe to say that this restructuring of the consonant system was complete by the second century A.D. The triangular consonant system

$$f$$
$$p \quad v$$

is an unusual one, and it is natural to ask whether b, d, g really existed in late Koine Greek, giving a rectangular consonant system

$$p \quad f$$
$$b \quad v$$

Numerous loan-words, particularly those from Latin, contained b, d and g; and they may have arisen as combinatory variants, as they do in modern Greek. But the question of the phonemic status of b, d, g is still not settled in regard to modern Greek, so we can scarcely be expected to answer it for late Koine. The evidence of the Coptic alphabet, in which the Greek letters with their conventional pronunciation were supplemented by a series of new letters for phonemes existing in late Egyptian but not in Koine Greek, ought to throw light on this and other problems of post-classical Greek phonology. But Coptic orthography is itself very variable, there were radical differences between the dialects of Coptic, which we cannot always grasp, and in any case we do not really know how Coptic was pronounced in antiquity: the traditional pronunciation of the Coptic church today may be misleading. In particular the pronunciation of ϴ φ χ as voiceless aspirates probably reflects Egyptian rather than post-Ptolemaic Greek phonology.[6]

The sonants l m n r remained unchanged. With the pronunciation of ζ as z, a new phonetic opposition between s and z arose. Whether the medieval and modern Greek affricate pair ts, dz existed in late Koine is not clear: and in any case their phonemic status in Modern Greek is still a matter of dispute. This radical restructuring of the phonology of the language took place largely without anyone noticing it. Yet its effects upon the structure of the language at other levels were wide-ranging and profound, as will be seen.

MORPHOLOGY

From its earliest period the Koine avoided certain morphological patterns of Attic. The dual was given up in nouns, pronouns, adjectives and verbs. Certain anomalous substantives were replaced by synonyms; this was particularly the case with monosyllabic substantives, in which the distinction between stem and termination was not as clear as was usual in Greek. Thus:

ναῦς, νηός or νεώς was replaced by πλοῖον (the only word for 'ship' in the N.T., though ναῦς occurs in the Septuagint)
οἶς, οἰός 'sheep' was replaced by πρόβατον
ἀμνός, ἀρνός 'lamb' „ ἀμνός, ἀμνοῦ
ὖς, ὑός 'pig' „ χοῖρος
ὕδωρ, ὕδατος 'water' „ νηρόν (νεαρόν)
κλείς, κλειδός 'key' „ κλειδίον
οὖς, ὠτός 'ear' „ ὠτίον

The Attic forms νεώς, νεῷ 'temple', λεώς, λεῷ 'people' were replaced by the Panhellenic forms ναός, λαός. κέρας, κέρως 'horn' and κρέας, κρέως 'meat' were replaced by κρέας, κρέατος and κρέας, κρέατος. There was much analogical tidying up of adjectives, especially those in which the pattern of declension was complicated by the effects of Attic vowel contraction. So for ὑγιής, ὑγιᾶ 'healthy' we find ὑγιής, ὑγιῆ, for ἐνδεής, ἐνδεᾶ, 'lacking', ἐνδεής, ἐνδεῆ.

Anomalous comparative and superlative forms were more and more replaced by forms in -τερος, -τατος. Thus ταχύτερος replaced θάσσων 'quicker' and ταχύτατος τάχιστος 'quickest': but this process was never completely carried out in Koine, and many anomalous comparatives remained in use.

Athematic verbs were to some extent replaced by thematic, thus δεικνύω replaced δείκνυμι 'show': but ἵημι, ἵστημι, τίθημι and δίδωμι remained in full use. The anomalous paradigm οἶδα, οἶσθα, οἶδε, ἴσμεν, ἴστε, ἴσασι 'know' was replaced by οἶδα, οἶδας, οἶδε, οἴδαμεν, οἴδατε, οἴδασι. ἦν, ἦσθα, ἦν 'was' tended to be replaced by ἤμην, ἦσο, ἦτο, but this process never extended to the standardised literary Koine. Weak aorist endings from the beginning tended to replace those of the strong aorist – εἶπα, εἶπας 'said' is already found in Attic. But this process was only slowly carried through completely, and is not fully reflected in literary Koine: ἔφθασα 'anticipated, arrived' and ἀνέγνωσα 'read' replace ἔφθην and ἀνέγνων but ἦλθα 'went', ἔλαβα 'got' were 'vulgarisms'. At the same time there was mutual interaction between the imperfect indicative and the weak aorist indicative: ἔγραψες 'wrote' and ἔγραφας are both found as analogical formations: ἔγραφαν replaces ἔγραφον in the 3rd plural, etc. -σαν, itself in origin an Attic innovation in athematic aorists such as ἔθεσαν for ἔθεν, is rapidly extended to the 3rd plural of all secondary indicative tenses, leading to forms like ἐγράφοσαν 'wrote', ἤλθοσαν 'went', ἠξιοῦσαν 'requested' etc. Middle futures of active verbs are early replaced by active forms, thus ἀκούσω, ὀμόσω replace ἀκούσομαι 'will hear', ὀμοῦμαι 'will swear'. This is part of a general reorganisation of the original three voices, active, middle and passive as two. So middle aorists tend to be replaced by passive: ἀπεκρίθην replaces ἀπεκρινάμην 'answered', less frequently ἐγενήθην replaces ἐγενόμην 'became'.

DEVELOPMENT OF KOINE

These features of the early Koine, most of which can be paralleled in Attic or other early dialects, and which were largely established by the time the N.T. texts were written, were only the beginning of a more radical restructuring of the verb system which we can trace in subliterary texts of the Roman and early Byzantine period. This was partly occasioned by the phonological changes described in an earlier paragraph, which resulted in λέγομεν and λέγωμεν (pres. indic. and pres. subj.), λύσει and λύσῃ (fut. indic. and aorist subj.) and many other pairs of forms coinciding. But apart from phonological considerations, there were also structural pressures at work. In ancient Greek differences of aspect and differences of tense did not necessarily coincide; in the Koine they tended more and more to do so. And the distinctions of aspect, which in ancient Greek were many-dimensional, tended in the Koine to be reduced to a single pair of polar opposites. Whatever be the relative importance attributed to the factors, the result by late antiquity was a drastic reorganisation of the verb system.

The main features of this reorganisation, some of which have been alluded to in the earlier part of this chapter are:

(1) The reduction of the three voices of classical Greek to two. Although many of the uses of the middle voice survived in κοινή – and even in modern Greek – from the morphological point of view the distinction between middle and passive is eliminated.

(2) The fusion of perfect and aorist. Perfect forms continue to appear in late κοινή texts, but they are used side by side with and in equivalence to aorist forms. It is sometimes hard to tell whether one is dealing with an aorist in -κα or with an irregularly reduplicated perfect. In medieval Greek, as we shall see, the confusion becomes complete. The perfect forms are 'desystematised', the first step in their elimination. This is the completion of a process, the first stages of which can already be observed in classical Greek.[7]

(3) The optative disappears as a separate category, except in a few fossilised usages, which are becoming lexical rather than grammatical. This is hardly a result of phonetic changes, as optative forms of thematic verbs remained phonetically distinct from indicative/subjunctive forms until at least the tenth century. The functions of the optative are taken over by the subjunctive, and by various periphrastic constructions.[8]

(4) Athematic verbs in -μι are replaced by thematic forms in -ω. The end result of this is to leave only two types of present, those in ⟵ω and those in -ῶ: distinctions, within the latter type are in process of elimination. The most tenacious of the -μι verbs is εἰμί: but even εἰμί tends to be replaced by a middle form εἶμαι, and the anomalous ἐστί, εἰσί by forms based on ἔνι, which was originally not a verbal form at all. On this see p. 70. However, some of the forms seem to have remained in living usage side by side with their surrogates in ⟵ω or -ῶ until the end of the period under discussion, e.g. John Moschos still makes large use of ἵημι, ἵστημι, τίθημι, δίδωμι.

(5) The present subjunctive coincides formally with the present indicative. The coincidence in pronunciation of λύεις and λύῃς, λύει and λύῃ, λύομεν and λύωμεν leads to the substitution of λύετε for λύητε and λύουσι for λύωσι. The aorist subjunctive, which undergoes the same changes, often coincides with the future indicative. However, the subjunctive remains functionally distinct from the indicative, since they can never both occur in the same context.

(6) The future tense, though continuing to survive in living speech, and maintained by the literary tradition, tends more and more to be replaced by a series of periphrases, which are discussed below, pp. 40, 82–3. In so far as these involve the infinitive, a distinction of aspect begins to arise within the future tense, according to whether the present or the aorist infinitive is used. This decay of the future is only in part explicable on phonetic grounds, e.g. by the coincidence of future indicative and aorist subjunctive in many verbs. The main factor is the restructuring of the verb system on the basis of two aspects and two only, each with its own distinct theme. The old future did not fit into this new system, and was hence more and more replaced in living speech by forms which did.[9]

(7) Sigmatic aorists more and more replace the non-sigmatic aorists of classical Greek, e.g. ἔνειμα 'distributed' is replaced by ἐνέμησα.

(8) Certain simplifications of the personal endings of verbal forms take place, of which the principal are the spread of -σαν in the third person plural of imperfects and aorists, and the replacement of -ον by -ε in the aorist imperative (not in Pontic).

Side by side with these changes, and in part determined by them, there appear a series of periphrastic verb forms, mostly formed with the verbs εἰμί 'am' and ἔχω 'have' together with infinitives or participles. These provide replacements for old forms which have been 'desystematised', such as the future, and facilitate the expression of the dual aspect system of late κοινή. These do not form a well-organised system in the period under discussion. Alternative patterns are found coexisting, and there is a great deal of uncertainty and imprecision. The main patterns of periphrastic conjugation which appear in late κοινή are:

(1) εἰμί (ἦν) + present participle active, competing with present and imperfect indicative. This construction occurs occasionally in classical Greek, but becomes much more frequent in the κοινή. Desire to emphasise the notion of continuity is probably the main motivating factor. But the opposition between continuous and momentary action is one of those expressed by the distinction between present and aorist theme in late κοινή, medieval and modern Greek. So the periphrasis with the present participle never succeeds in replacing the present and imperfect indicative in κοινή Greek. However, the construction continues in use

during the medieval period as an alternative expression of continuity, and only disappears when the present participle is lost. In Tsakonian, in contradistinction to common Greek, the participial periphrasis did replace the present and imperfect indicative form. In that dialect we have as present indicative:

$$\text{ἔμι ὁροῦ 'I see'}$$
$$\text{ἔσσι ,,}$$
$$\text{ἔννι ,,} \qquad \text{etc.}$$

as imperfect indicative:

$$\text{ἔμα ὁροῦ 'I saw'}$$
$$\text{ἔσα ,,}$$
$$\text{ἔκη ,,} \qquad \text{etc.}$$

while the corresponding subjunctive form is not periphrastic.[10] Occasionally εἰμί + aorist participle is found as a continuous present in late Koine texts. This is indicative of the beginning of the break down of the system of participles, which took place in the following period.

(2) εἰμί + perfect participle active replaces the missing perfect, and expresses present state resulting from past action, e.g. εἰμὶ τεθαρρηκώς 'I am confident'. The same function is often performed by εἰμί + aorist participle, the aorist and perfect forms being considered equivalents. Common in classical Greek is subjunctive and optative, this periphrasis is extended by Koine to the indicative, but never becomes really common. The aorist participle is commoner than the perfect, and the auxiliary verb is most often imperfect, i.e. the periphrasis is a pluperfect substitute.

(3) εἰμί + perfect participle passive, or less frequently aorist participle passive, similarly replaces the medio-passive perfect.

(4) ἔχω + an active participle – usually aorist – furnishes another perfect-equivalent in transitive verbs, e.g. ἔχω τελευτήσας 'I have completed'. This pattern is rare in late Koine and hardly occurs at all in medieval Greek.

(5) A similar function is performed by ἔχω + perfect participle passive. This unclassical periphrasis occurs only occasionally in Koine and is not frequent in Byzantine writers. Its period of greatest extension is probably in early modern Greek, cf. p. 97.

(6) ἔχω + infinitive, on the other hand, is a future-equivalent extremely common in late texts which reflect the spoken Greek of the time. The infinitive is most often aorist, but the present is also found. Less frequently εἶχον (εἶχα) + infinitive is found serving as a potential or conditional form, replacing the optative + ἄν of classical Greek.[11]

(7) Another future-equivalent, originally with a somewhat different nuance – will as opposed to obligation – is provided by θέλω + infinitive.

(8) A further group of future-equivalents is provided by ὀφείλω 'owe' + infinitive, μέλλω 'am about to, intend' + infinitive, ἔσομαι + present participle (cf. §(1) above) and ἵνα + subjunctive. There are corresponding conditional periphrases formed by ὤφειλον (ὤφειλα) + infinitive and ἔμελλον + infinitive.

(9) συμβαίνει 'it happens' + infinitive, εὑρίσκομαι 'I find myself' + present participle etc. provide further quasi-modal verbal periphrases.

What emerges from all this is that the late Koine verb has only two themes, corresponding to two opposed aspects. All other aspectual distinctions are expressed by periphrases. It has two voices, active and medio-passive, and two moods, which in the case of the present theme are not morphologically distinct. The present theme forms a present and past indicative, a subjunctive and an imperative, the aorist theme forms a past indicative, a subjunctive and an imperative. Futurity is either expressed by the context, or by one or other of a series of periphrases, and the distinction of aspect begins to penetrate the future. The old perfect has been replaced by a series of periphrases, and its forms, where they survive, function as aorists or as elements in clichés, such as formulae of signature. The system of non-personal verbal forms, the infinitives and participles, is preserved with little change, except that future infinitives and participles virtually vanish, and perfect infinitives and participles become rare, and are generally equivalent to the corresponding aorist forms.

It is very hard to date any of these changes, owing to the nature of our evidence, and the inevitable contamination of any written text by the purist language. In any case many of them are only extensions of features already existing in classical Greek. What is important is not this or that individual innovation, but the new system. And, as always in language, old and new systems existed side by side in living speech for a long time, until the distinctive features of the old became 'desystematised' and thus condemned to disappear – except in so far as in Greek the prestige of the traditional purist language of writing and fine speech conferred upon some of them a factitious, zombie-like life. An example of the actual state of the language is provided by the *Spiritual Meadow* of John Moschos. Influences of the literary tradition and above all of the New Testament are present, but on the whole this text is fairly representative of the spoken Greek of the sixth century of our era. This is the position regarding the expression of futurity.

There are only fifty-five true future forms. The usual form for the expressions of futurity is the present indicative, the next most frequent the aorist subjunctive, both active and passive – an example of both forms together is κοιμηθῶ εἰς τὴν ὁδὸν τοῦ λέοντος καὶ τρώγει με 'I shall lie down in the path of the lion and he will eat me' (2960 C). The occasional optatives expressing futurity are due to the feeling that the optative is a 'refined' equivalent of the subjunctive. In addition the following types of periphrasis are found: ἔσομαι + present participle, μέλλω + present or aorist infinitive, θέλω + aorist infinitive, ἔχω + aorist infinitive, ἔξομαι + aorist infinitive, ὀφείλων + aorist infinitive = future participle. This state of affairs indicates the instability of the structure of the language, which was complicated but not fundamentally modified by the existence of an archaising written language enjoying great prestige.

Another striking example is provided by the use of the optative in the New Testament. There are only forty-one examples in main clauses (more or less, since the existence of variant readings complicates the situation). Of these, thirty-eight are wishing optatives (all but one in the third person) and fifteen of these are instances of the cliché μὴ γένοιτο 'may it not be', which still survives as a lexical item in modern Greek; the remaining three are potential optatives with ἄν. There are eleven optatives in subordinate clauses introduced by εἰ, of which four are indirect questions; there are probably no final optatives; there are a few indirect optatives in indirect questions – sometimes accompanied by ἄν – but none in indirect statements. The regular conditional construction εἰ + opt., followed by opt. + ἄν, does not occur in the N.T. It is clear that the optative was not a feature of the everyday speech of the N.T. writers, though they were familiar with certain of its uses through their contact with the literary tradition, and preserved some 'desystematised' optatives in phrases which were becoming lexical units rather than syntactic constructions.

In the sphere of nominal syntax, the most striking change in the period under discussion is the beginning of the elimination of the dative case. The Greek dative case fulfilled the role not only of the Indo-European dative, but also those of the locative and the instrumental. This multiplicity of significances led to ambiguity, and in classical Greek alternating patterns began to emerge – διά+genitive in the instrumental sense etc. In Koine Greek this process was carried much further. The locative of ἐν+dative was replaced by εἰς+accusative, in accordance with the Greek tendency to confuse motion towards and rest in something. By the first century A.D. the process was well advanced, and a choice existed between the two modes of expression, as the following parallel passages in the Gospels demonstrate:

Mark	*Matthew*	*Luke*
xiii,16	xxiv,18	xvii,31
ὁ εἰς τὸν ἀγρὸν μὴ	ὁ ἐν τῷ ἀγρῷ	ὁ ἐν τῷ ἀγρῷ
ἐπιστρεψάτω εἰς	μὴ ἐπιστρεψάτω	ὁμοίως μὴ ἐπιστρε-
τὰ ὀπίσω	εἰς τὰ ὀπίσω	ψάτω εἰς τὰ ὀπίσω
xiii,9	x,17	
παραδώσουσιν ὑμᾶς	καί ἐν ταῖς	
εἰς συνέδρια καὶ εἰς	συναγωγαῖς αὐτῶν	
συναγωγὰς δαρήσεσθε	μαστιγώσουσιν ὑμᾶς	
i,12	iv,1	iv,1
καὶ εὐθύς τό Πνεῦμα	τότε ὁ ᾽Ιησοῦς	ἤγετο ἐν τῷ
αὐτὸν ἐκβάλλει εἰς	ἀνήχθη εἰς τὴν	Πνεύματι ἐν τῇ
τὴν ἔρημον	ἔρημον ὑπὸ τοῦ	ἐρήμῳ
	Πνεύματος	

As the last example shows, one of the signs of the growing confusion is the erroneous use of ἐν+dative of motion towards. Later vulgar texts of the period under discussion more and more frequently use εἰς+accusative of rest, which was evidently the usage of the spoken language.

The instrumental use of the dative was replaced by a series of constructions, all of which turn up occasionally in classical Greek. The first was ἐν+dative, the next διά+genitive, which appear to have been the common usage of later spoken Koine, as evidenced by non-literary papyri, and finally from the fourth century on μετά+genitive. By the tenth century, to glance ahead a moment, all prepositions governed the accusative case, and μετά + accusative first makes its appearance in an instrumental sense alongside of μετά + genitive in the *Book of Ceremonies* of Constantine Porphyrogenitus. The modern Greek μὲ + accusative is the descendant of this construction.

The dative form survived longest in the sense of the pure dative – indirect object or person interested. But we find first the accusative, and later the genitive, of personal pronouns replacing the dative from the first century B.C. on in non-literary papyri, in such phrases as γράφομαί σε 'I write to you' (81 B.C.), ἀποστελῶ σε 'I send to you' (1 B.C.), σὲ δίδω 'I give you' (late fourth century), πέμψον με τὸ πλοῖον 'send me the boat' (late fifteenth century), καθως εἶπες με 'as you told me' (6–7th century), δώσω σου 'I shall give you' (46 B.C.), ἔπεμψά σου 'I sent to you' (346), εἴρηκά σου 'I told you' (end of fourth century), ἀγόρασόν μου 'buy for me' (second century). This construction spreads to substantives in the early centuries of our era, as is evidenced by such phrases as these in papyrus letters: ἔδωκα οὖν Μαξίμου 'I gave to Maximus' (c. 340), παράσχον Θεοδώρου 'furnish to Theodore' (seventh century), and by the use of dative and genitive forms side by side in papyri and inscriptions; e.g. Ἑλένη Πετεχῶντος τῷ ἀδελφῷ χαίρειν 'Helen to her brother Petechôs greetings' (3rd century), τῷ γλυκυτάτω μου ἀνδρὶ Πολυχρονίου 'to my dearest husband Polychronios', ἀνέστησα ἐμαυτῷ καὶ Εἴας τῆς συμβίου 'I set up [this] to myself and to Eia my wife'. Δόξα πατρὶ καὶ υἱοῦ καὶ ἁγίου πνεύματος 'glory to the Father and to the Son and to the Holy Ghost'. It is not until the ninth or tenth century that we find clear cases of substitution of genitive or accusative for dative proper in literary texts, as we shall see in the next chapter. Modern Greek is divided in its usage. The northern dialects use the accusative, the southern dialects, which form the basis of common demotic, the genitive.

Thus we see that during the period under discussion the dative forms of noun, pronoun and adjective ceased to have a clear function in the structure of the language, became used more and more erratically, and were probably maintained in the consciousness of speaking mainly by the influence of the purist language. In the subsequent period, they disappeared from living use.[12]

During the period under review a development of the noun declension pattern took place, which cannot be explained on phonetic grounds. Various analogical influences have been suggested, but the explanation still remains uncertain. Neuter

substantives in -ιον and -ίον lost their final vowel, and came to end
in -ιν and -ίν. Examples are common in inscriptions and papyri
from the second century on, e.g. ἐνόρμιν 'mooring' (A.D. 115),
ἡμιλίτριν 'half-pound' (A.D. 265), φυλακτήριν 'amulet' (A.D. 149),
ἐπαύλιν 'shelter', ἐπιστόλιν 'letter', ζωίδιν 'beast', πεπόνιν
'melon', πιττάκιν 'tablet'. They did not in the Koine drive out
the longer forms, but were alternatives to them. At the same
time masculine proper names in -ιος similarly lost their final
vowel. Ἀντώνιος becoming Ἀντώνις and so on. This caused
these nouns to pass over to the class in -ης, -ην, -η, itself the result
of a conflation of a- stem nouns in -ης like Χαρμίδης and con-
sonant-stem nouns like Ἀριστοτέλης, which had begun in
classical times. There is little sign of a similar change in common
nouns or adjectives in -ιος.

KOINE VOCABULARY

The vocabulary was extended during the κοινή period by derivation and by borrowing. Certain suffixes, including new suffixes
first appearing in post-classical Greek, became extremely productive. These include:

(a) Agent nouns
   -της
   -εύς
   -εύτης
   -άριος (of Latin origin)
   -ᾶς
   -τρια
   -ισσα

(b) Verbal abstracts
   -σις
   -σία (which tends to replace -σις in later κοινή)
   -μός
   -μα

The original semantic distinctions between these tend to be
eliminated.

(c) Abstract nouns of quality
   -ία
   -ότης

(d) Nouns of place
-εών
-τήριον

(e) Nouns of instrument
-άριον (of Latin origin)
-τρον

(f) Diminutives
-ιον
-ίδιον
-άριον

(g) Adjectives of material
-ινος

(h) Adjectives of quality
-ικός
-ιος (the last three tend to become semantically equivalent)

(i) Verbal adjectives
-τός
-σιμος

(j) Miscellaneous Adjectives
-ιανός (of Latin origin)

(k) Verbs
-έω
-όω
-εύω
-άζω
-ίζω

At the same time some derivational suffixes which are productive in classical Greek and early Koine, cease to be productive in later Koine, e.g. -τήρ, -αινα, -σύνη (which again becomes productive in Modern Greek), -θρον, -θρα, -τρα, -οῦς, -ύνω. It will be noted that among the productive suffixes are some of Latin origin. Speakers who were familiar with these in Latin loan-words used them to form derivatives from Greek stems. Thus we find μηχανάριος, προβολάριος, ἀχυράριος, προθηκάριος, γραφιάριον, στρατιωτάριον, μαγιανός. [13]

The main source of loan-words in the Koine of the Roman empire was Latin. Military and administrative terms were adopted in large numbers, as well as names of measures, trade objects and artefacts of western origin. These Latin loan-words entered

Greek via the spoken language or the sub-literary written language
of quartermasters' stores, tax-collectors' offices and merchants'
counting-houses. They were, with a very few exceptions, es-
chewed by literary Greek of the period. It is significant that St
Luke, who has rather more literary pretensions than the Synop-
tics, often replaces a Latin loan-word in their text by a Greek
equivalent, e.g.

for κεντυρίων 'centurion' he writes ἑκατοντάρχης
κῆνσος 'census'   φόρος
μόδιος 'bushel'   σκεῦος
κοδράντης 'farthing'   λεπτόν
τίτλος 'little'   ἐπιγραφή

The great majority of these Latin loan-words are substantives
or adjectives, e.g. ἀκτουάριος, βενεφικιάριος, λανάριος, κοδράντης, τροῦλλα, φορμαλεία, τρακτευτής, κλάσσῃ, κουστωδία,
βρακαρία, ὁσπίτιον, μανούβριον, κολλήγιον, ἀρμάριον, κιβάριον,
βαλανάριον, λωρήκιον (formed with Greek diminutive suffix from
Latin lorica), δησέρτωρ, κουράτωρ, κοντουβερνάλιος, ὀφικιά-
λιος, πραιτώριος, καγκελλωτός, δηπουτᾶτος, πλουμαριᾶτος,
καρτιανός, μαγιστριανός.

Many of these words remained as living elements of the Greek
language long after there had ceased to be any significant Greco-
Latin bilingualism. The fact that Greek derivational suffixes are
attached to Latin stems, e.g. πορτᾶς, παστιλλᾶς, ἐξπελλευτής,
and that certain Latin suffixes were used to form derivatives from
Greek stems, shows that these loan-words were not felt to be
alien elements in the language, though they were avoided by the
literary language.

It is to be noted that there are very few verbs among the Latin
loan-words. Greek finds it difficult to borrow verbs, because a
Greek verb requires two themes – and in Koine it might still re-
quire a perfect theme as well. Hence any borrowed verb has to
be made to fit into a pattern of complementary themes. This can
only be done by giving it one of a group of productive verbal
suffixes, e.g. -ίζω, -εύω. But these were felt to be characteristic
of denominative verbs, hence they could not readily be used to
adapt Latin verbs to the needs of Greek morphology. So we find
Greek verbs formed from Latin nominal stems, e.g. ἀννωνεύω,
δηληγατεύω, πραιδεύω, στατιωνίζω, but few at this period
formed from Latin verbal stems. Among the rare exceptions are

ἀπλικεύω, βιγλεύω, and ρογεύω, the two latter in due course giving rise to the deverbative nouns βίγλα and ρόγα. Latin nouns and adjectives could generally be fitted into Greek declension patterns without difficulty. But we find a number of analogical modifications taking place. Changes of gender are common, e.g. *limes* > λίμιτον, *expeditus* > ἐξπέδιτον (analogy of στρατόπεδον?). *denarius* > δηνάριον, *camisia* > καμίσιον. And the gender of a loan-word is sometimes uncertain, e.g. κανδηλάβρα and κανδήλαβρον, κούκουμος and κουκούμιον, λῶρις, λῶρον and λώριον, μάκελλος, μακέλλη and μάκελλον, μεμβράνα and μέμβρανον. The tendency to replace masculines and feminines by neuter diminutives is common to inherited Greek words and to Latin loan-words. There are often analogical changes of suffix, e.g. *patronus* > πατρών, *cohors* > κόρτη, *magister* > μαγιστώρ, *fabrica* > φάβρικα, φαβρική, φάβριξ. Occasionally hybrid Greco-Latin forms are found, due to popular etymologising, e.g. κλεισοῦρα (defile) from *clausura*+κλείω, συμψέλιον from *subsellium*+σύν.[14]

As a result both of its development of its own resources by derivation and composition, and of its capacity to absorb loanwords, mainly from Latin, and to build upon them by derivation and composition, the vocabulary of Koine Greek is extraordinarily large. Arguments from silence prove nothing in such matters. But an examination of a few pages of an ancient Greek lexicon, e.g. that of Liddell-Scott-Jones, will show that the majority of the words there recorded were first attested in the period under review. The vocabulary of Greek, then as in the middle ages, and to a slightly less extent today, was open-ended, in that new derivatives and compounds were freely formed as the occasion required.[15]

As well as the creation or borrowing of new words Greek augmented its lexical resources by attaching new meanings to old words. The well-established literary tradition ensured that the old meanings survived in use, at any rate among the literate, side by side with the new meanings. Examples of this semantic enrichment are:

ἀνακλίνομαι	'to be leant against something' – 'to recline at table'
ἀντίληψις	'laying hold of, support, defence, claim' – 'mental apprehension'
ἄριστον	'morning meal' – 'meal in general'

διάφορον	'difference, disagreement, balance, expenses' – 'cash, ready money'
δῶμα	'house (poetic)' – 'roof'
ἔξοδος	'expedition, procession', 'way out, end' – 'expenses'
ἐρωτάω	'ask, enquire' – 'beg, entreat'
κηδεία	'connexion by marriage' – 'funeral, mourning'
κοίμησις	'sleep' – 'death'
μνημεῖον	'souvenir, memorial' – 'tomb'
ὀψάριον	'delicacy' – 'fish'
παιδεύω	'educate' – 'punish'
παρακαλέω	'summon, invite' – 'comfort, console'
παρρησία	'free speech' – 'confidence'
πτῶμα	'fall' – 'corpse, ruins of a building'
ῥύμη	'impetus, rush, charge' – 'street'
στενοχωρία	'confined space' – 'difficulty, distress'
στόμαχος	'gullet' – 'stomach'
φθάνω	'anticipate' – 'arrive'
χρηματίζω	'negotiate, give response (of an oracle)' – 'be called'

In the field of syntax the period under discussion is one of transition. The distinction between verbal sentence and nominal sentence, was maintained throughout Greek from Homer to the present day. The non-personal verbal forms, infinitive and participle, were still preserved, though alternatives appeared to most of the constructions in which they were used.[16] In particular ἵνα + subjunctive appears as an alternative to most uses of the infinitive other than that in indirect speech. The accentual rhythm of some of the Hymns of Romanos (sixth century) indicates that in its purely subordinating capacity, as a mere marker for the subjunctive, which was often morphologically indistinguishable from the indicative, ἵνα was beginning to be pronounced ἰνά – the ancestor of the Modern Greek subjunctive marker νά.[17] As the system of three moods – indicative, subjunctive and optative – which classical Greek had inherited from Indo-European was replaced by a dual system of two moods, indicative and subjunctive, a great many of the distinctions which the classical language made in the syntax of the complex sentence became impossible. This is reflected in the literary language of the period – even in that which seeks to imitate Attic – by a looseness in modal usage. Subjunctives and optatives are used side by side in similar contexts, indicatives appear in situations which in classical Greek required the subjunctive or optative, and so on.

In particular it is clear that the difference between generic and particular relative and temporal clauses was no longer made; ὅταν, ἐπειδάν etc. are used from now on with the indicative. With the loss of the potential optative a new series of periphrastic constructions appears, in which the imperfect of an auxiliary verb – ἔχω or μέλλω or θέλω or ὀφείλω – is followed by the infinitive. The negatives οὐ and μή are more and more used in such a way that οὐ negatives indicatives, μή all other moods. Parataxis with καί is often substituted for hypotaxis: e.g. Τί μοι παρέχεις καὶ παρέχω σοι τίποτε τὰ μέγιστα σοῦ εὐεργετοῦν 'what will you give me that I should give you something of the greatest benefit to you' (John Moschos).[18]

THE ATTICIST MOVEMENT AND ITS AFTERMATH

Towards the end of the first century B.C. we find teachers of grammar and rhetoric preaching a new doctrine – that language must not be allowed to change and develop, since all change is decadence, that the only 'correct' Greek is that used by classical Attic writers, and the Koine, both as the common spoken language of all classes and in its literary form must be rejected as a product of ignorance, debasement and vulgarity. In the ensuing two centuries this movement gathered weight and influence, came to dominate the teaching of Greek in schools, and greatly influenced all literary prose, leading to a conscious imitation of ancient linguistic patterns, real or imagined, and a deliberate rejection of the living and developing language as a vehicle of formal speech and literature. It was in this way that a beginning was made of the diglossy which has been so marked a feature of Greek throughout its subsequent history.

The causes were probably many, operating at different levels of consciousness. We are not in a position today, unfortunately, to determine to which of them the enormous success of this purist movement was due. Among the main factors must be counted:

(1) The growing discrepancy between contemporary living speech and the language of the literary texts upon which education was based. As the development of Koine Greek proceeded this created an ever more pressing problem for teachers.
(2) It is probable that the beginnings of a new dialect differentiation were taking place within Koine though there is very little direct evidence of this.

(3) Teachers of rhetoric, in reacting against a flowery and ornate style current in the first century B.C., urged closer imitation of classical models. Imitation of their style soon brought with it imitation of their linguistic patterns. This occurs particularly easily in Greek, in which the linguistic form used is largely a function of the situation, i.e. in works of literature a function of the literary genre.

(4) Reaction to Roman domination led, particularly after the Mithridatic War and Sulla's regime of repression in Greece and Asia Minor, to a new nostalgic harking back to the great days of Greek freedom. Teachers of rhetoric handled almost exclusively themes from the period between the Persian Wars and Alexander the Great, and turned their backs on their own age. Classical writers were the only models worthy of imitation. If only men spoke and wrote like their great forebears they might somehow recreate the lost glory of Greece.

(5) A society sharply divided into classes needs status symbols. English readers need hardly be reminded of the role which language can play in indicating a speaker's class-position. So in the ancient world the living developing speech of the common people, who had no literary education, was despised by those wealthy enough to have had a literary education, and who found in the distinction between their purist speech and that of the masses just the kind of symbol they sought.

We find a body of didactic literature growing up, prescribing what one must and must not say, at all levels from phonology to syntax. The prescriptions are usually particular, not general, in the form: 'Say A, not B'. Obsolete words were resuscitated from literary texts, and the Koine replacements anathematised as 'incorrect', 'vulgar', 'shocking'. Obsolete inflections were given preference over those in every day use, obsolete Attic forms like the dual and the so-called Attic declension were given a fresh though factitious lease of life, obsolete meanings were declared to be the only correct ones. A distinction is often drawn between 'Attic' and 'Hellenic' usage, the former referring to the obsolete words or forms found in classical prose texts, the latter to post-classical Koine forms in living use. Occasionally more complex classifications are attempted.

The use of the 'Attic' words and forms become a mark of culture and of literary acceptability. The criterion of correct usage is whether a word or form is attested in a limited body of literary texts composed five centuries earlier. Ancient authority replaced spontaneity. There is a character in Athenaeus' *Deipnosophists* nicknamed Κειτούκειτος, because his invariable question when any new topic is introduced is to enquire if the name of it is attested in the corpus of classical literature or not – κεῖται ἢ οὐ κεῖται. The normal relation of spoken and written language became reversed. Speech was to follow writing.

As direct evidence of the tenets of the Atticists we have a number of lexica laying down correct usage, and fragments from many other works of this kind incorporated in commentaries on classical texts. As indirect evidence we have the practice of writers.

No prose literature of the first century A.D. was unaffected by the Atticist movement.[19] In a society in which education was widespread, and in which it was education and way of life rather than racial origin which made a Greek a Greek, it could not be otherwise. But there were variations in degree and quality of influence. Professional rhetoricians like Herodes Atticus, the Philostrati, Aelian, Aelius Aristides and Dio Chrysostom try to avoid scrupulously Koine words and forms, and scatter Attic expressions, culled from lexica, over their pages in the vain attempt to produce a pastiche of the language and style of half a millennium earlier. Lucian is a careful Atticist, although he mocks the excesses of his more pedantic contemporaries in his *Lexiphanes* and his *Rhetorum praeceptor*. Writers who have much to say, such as Plutarch and Galen, observe many of the general precepts of the Atticists, but avoid the slavish imitation in detail of ancient models and are ready to draw on the spoken language of their own day, especially in the matter of vocabulary. Galen has some interesting observations on matters of language. He condemns 'the practitioners of false learning' for calling by the term ῥάφανος – used by the Athenians 600 years earlier – a vegetable which all Greeks now call κράμβη 'cabbage'.[20] He mocks at the fussy Atticists, who call a bodyguard κοιτωνήτης instead of σωματοφύλαξ.[21] In a long defence of his own language and style against a critic he says that he uses the so-called 'common dialect' (κοινὴ διάλεκτος). This, be it a variety of Attic or not, certainly includes elements from other dialects: he asks his critic to maintain this dialect in its purity and not to contaminate it with Cilician, Syrian, Galatian – or Athenian – borrowings. He adds that he had learnt a particularly pure Greek from his father.[22] Whatever we are to make of this outburst, it is evidence of the difficulty which men felt in choosing the correct linguistic form for public or formal utterances. The young Marcus Aurelius, writing in Greek to his mother, asks her to excuse him for any incorrect or barbarous or unapproved or un-Attic word which he may have carelessly used.[23] The same Marcus Aurelius in the philosophical diary which he kept as emperor, is no longer concerned with such trivialities, but writes in literary Koine – the *Meditations* were not written for publication – and the Stoic philosophers of the Roman empire in general despised the preoccupations of rhetoricians.

In view of the conscious effort which Atticism called for, it is not surprising that Atticising writers continuously fail in their purpose. Either they admit Koine forms censured by the grammarians – this is too common to call for illustration – or they over-compensate and produce false Atticisms, hypercorrect forms which never existed in classical Attic. The literature of this period is full of middle voices where Attic uses in fact the active, of wrongly used datives, e.g. of duration of time, of optatives in conditional clauses introduced by ἐάν or in final clauses in primary sequence. At the level of morphology we find such monstrosities as ῥίν for ῥίς 'nose', on the analogy of the genitive ῥινός, συνεωρτάζομεν 'we celebrated together' with a false Attic augment after the pattern of ἑώρακα, ἀγγελῆναι for ἀγγελθῆναι, aorists passive in -ην being felt to be more refined than those in -θην, ἐλῶ as future of αἱρέω, οἰσάμενος as aorist participle on the analogy of the future οἴσομαι, φνήσομαι from φύω, presumably on the analogy of ῥνήσομαι, στενάξειε, with an aorist optative termination attached to a present stem, ωρυγε for ὤρυξε, and so on. These men were attempting to write in a language which they knew imperfectly and they made blunders right and left. This has been one of the marks of Greek diglossy ever since.

To show the way in which the Atticists consciously rejected the living speech of their time, let us put side by side some well-known passages from the Gospels – which on the whole represent the spoken Greek of the first century A.D. remarkably well – with certain observations of the Atticist lexicographer Phrynichus (second half of the second century). It is to be borne in mind that Phrynichus is not commenting on the New Testament, which he had probably never heard of, but on the 'errors' made by his own pupils in literary composition.

New Testament

1. Πάτερ εὐχαριστῶ σοι.
John xi, 41

2. Ἆρον τὸν κράββατόν σου καὶ περιπάτει. Mark ii, 9

3. Εὐκολώτερόν ἐστι κάμηλον διὰ τρυπήματος ῥαφίδος διελθεῖν. Mat. xix, 24

4. Κρούσαντος δὲ αὐτοῦ τὴν θύραν. Acts xii, 3

5. Ὁμοία ἐστὶν βασιλεία τῶν οὐρανῶν κόκκῳ σινάπεως. Mat. xiii, 31

6. Βρέχει ἐπὶ δικαίους παὶ ἀδίκους. Mat. v, 45

7. Ἐκάμμυσαν τοὺς ὀφθαλμούς. Mat. xiii, 5

8. Τὸ θυγάτριόν μου ἐσχάτως ἔχει. Mark v, 23

9. Μακάριος ὅστις φάγεται ἄριστον. Luke xiv, 15

10. Ἀπελεύσονται οὗτοι εἰς κόλασιν αἰώνιον. Mat. xxv, 46

11. Ἐπὶ ὀλίγα ἦς πιστός. Mat. xxv, 21

12. Ὁ δὲ Παῦλος τοῖς ἀδελφοῖς ἀποταξάμενος ἐξέπλει. Acts xviii 21

13. Ἐδέετο δὲ αὐτοῦ ὁ ἀνήρ. Luke viii, 38

Phrynichus

Εὐχαριστεῖν οὐδεὶς τῶν δοκίμων εἶπεν, ἀλλὰ χάριν εἰδέναι. Σκίμπους λέγε, ἀλλὰ μὴ κράββατος.

Βελόνη καὶ βελονοπώλης ἀρχαῖα, ἡ δὲ ῥαφὶς τί ἐστιν οὐκ ἄν τις γνοίη.

Κροῦσαι τὴν θύραν ἴσως μέν που παραβεβίασται ἡ χρῆσις· ἄμεινον δὲ τὸ κόπτειν τὴν θύραν.

Σίναπι οὐ λεκτέον, νᾶπυ δέ.

Βρέχειν ἐπὶ τοῦ ὕειν . . . παντελῶς ἀποδοκιμαστέον τοὔνομα.

Καμμύει· τοσαύτη κακοδαιμονία περί τινάς ἐστι τῆς βαρβαρίας, ὥστ᾽ ἐπειδὴ Ἄλεξις κέχρηται τῷ καμμύειν ἠμελημένως ἐσχάτως, αἱρεῖσθαι καὶ αὐτοὺς οὕτω λέγειν, δέον ὡς οἱ ἄριστοι τῶν ἀρχαίων καταμύειν.

Ἐσχάτως ἔχει ἐπὶ τοῦ μοχθηρῶς ἔχει καὶ σφαλερῶς τάττουσιν οἱ σύρφακες.

Φάγομαι βάρβαρον. λέγε οὖν ἔδομαι καὶ κατέδομαι· τοῦτο γὰρ Ἀττικόν.

Ἀπελεύσομαι παντάπασι φυλάττου· οὔτε γὰρ οἱ δόκιμοι ῥήτορες, οὔτε ἡ ἀρχαία κωμῳδία, οὔτε Πλάτων κέχρηται τῇ φωνῇ· ἀντὶ δ᾽ αὐτοῦ τῷ ἄπειμι χρῶ καὶ τοῖς ὁμοειδέσιν ὡσαύτως.

Ἧς ἐν ἀγορᾷ σόλοικον. λέγε οὖν ἦσθα.

Ἀποτάσσομαί σοι ἔκφυλον πάνυ. χρὴ λέγειν ἀσπάζομαί σε· οὕτω γὰρ καὶ οἱ ἀρχαῖοι εὑρίσκονται λέγοντες ἐπειδὰν ἀπαλλάττωνται ἀλλήλων.

Ἐδέετο, ἐπλέετο. Ἰωνικὰ ταῦτα· ἡ δὲ Ἀττικὴ συνήθεια συναίρει, ἐδεῖτο, ἐπλεῖτο, ἐρρεῖτο.

The New Testament, we have seen, was written substantially in the spoken Greek of the time, though with varying degrees of literary pretension – Luke often 'corrects' what he finds in Mark, the Pauline epistles are more literary than the Gospels, the Apocalypse has so many linguistic anomalies and oddities that it seems likely that its author's knowledge of Greek was imperfect. The Christian writers of the earliest period, the so-called Apostolic Fathers, on the whole followed the N.T. model, and wrote as they spoke, with no regard for the precepts of pagan grammarians and rhetoricians, whom they despised. The *Shepherd* of Hermas is a monument of spoken Koine, as is also the *Didache*: Clement of Rome has occasional literary pretensions; the N.T. Apocrypha are largely written in the vulgar Greek of the time, and so on.[24] Some of the early saints' lives are similarly written in the spoken Greek of the time, with more or less strong N.T. influences. This might have become the pattern of Christian Greek literature, and the diglossy introduced by the Atticists might have been overcome. But Christian writers who aimed to convert cultivated pagans had to write – and presumably preach – in language acceptable to their readers. So we find the Christian apologists from the second century on writing in more or less Atticising Greek, i.e. accepting the fact of diglossy. Clement of Alexandria in the third century, writing both for his fellow-Christians and for the pagan world, uses the Atticising literary Greek of the time, just as he attempts to explain Christian doctrines in terms of Hellenic philosophy. As Christianity, at first largely confined to the lower classes, made headway among the cultivated upper classes of Greek-speaking society, the problem of an acceptable linguistic form became acute. The prestige which the archaising literary tongue enjoyed was enormous; it was the only kind of Greek taught in schools. The use of the spoken tongue on formal occasions was stigmatised as barbarous. The N.T., word of God though it might be, was not acceptable as a linguistic model to these new Christians. The church historian Socrates, writing of the emperor Julian's attempt to prevent Christians from teaching in schools, remarks that Holy Writ teaches us marvellous and divine doctrines, but does not teach us the art of literature so that we may answer those who attack the truth. The great fourth century fathers, most of them men with a traditional education, like Basil, Gregory of Nazianzus, John Chrysostom, all unhesitatingly rejected the spoken language of their time as a vehicle for writing and preaching, and chose the archaising literary language which was the lingua franca of the educated classes.[25] There is a story that an old woman once interrupted one of John Chrysostom's sermons to complain that she could not understand half of what he was saying, so remote was his language from that of the mass of the people. The preacher obligingly delivered the rest of his sermon, we are told, in the vulgar tongue. But he certainly never wrote in the vulgar tongue. These writers dealt with the charismatic prestige of the N.T. and the Septuagint by embodying words and expressions from these texts in their own archaising language like technical terms or quotations from a foreign tongue, i.e. at a purely lexical level, while rejecting the morphological and syntactical features of the Greek Bible.

This development sealed the fate of spoken Greek, endowed the purist language with a new prestige, and perpetuated the diglossy introduced by schoolmasters four centuries earlier. The language of the Fathers of the Church became that of almost all subsequent Greek literature for 1000 years. There was, it is true, an undercurrent of writing in a linguistic form making greater or lesser concessions to spoken Greek, but it remained a humble undercurrent. It comprised early saints' lives, tales of the desert fathers, world chronicles, and the like. It seems to have been largely written for monks. Monks were the only literate group in society which had not had a traditional classical education.

THE DECLINE OF THE ANCIENT DIALECTS

The spread of the Koine caused the general disappearance of the ancient dialects, and the new dialects which begin to appear in the late middle ages are all developments of Koine Greek, occasionally with certain residual influences from the ancient dialects (cf. Chapter 7). The detailed history of the decline of the dialects cannot be traced. Our principal source of information is inscriptions. These usually have something of an official character, and they are essentially the products of urban society – peasants do not set up inscribed slabs of stone. For what it is worth, the picture which emerges from a study of the inscriptions is this.[26]

Ionic, being closely akin to Attic and under strong Attic influence from the mid fifth century, was the first to yield to the pressure of Attic and the Attic-based Koine. From the beginning of the fourth century B.C. Attic forms are common in the inscriptions of Ionic cities of Asia Minor, the Cyclades, and Euboea, and by the end of the second or beginning of the first century B.C. their inscriptions are all in Koine. The Aeolic-speaking communities held out longer. The inscriptions of Pergamum are written in Koine from the third century, but dialect continued to appear in the inscriptions of Lesbos until the first century B.C.; Thessalian, Boeotian and North-West Greek did not last quite so long. The revival of Lesbian dialect in certain inscriptions in the second century A.D. is a piece of antiquarianism, and has nothing to do with the spoken tongue. Doric was most tenacious of all; especially in the Peloponnese and in Rhodes. In the late third and early second centuries B.C. the local dialects of the Peloponnese were replaced in official inscriptions by the Doric Koine of the Achaean League, which in its turn was replaced by common Hellenistic Koine after the dissolution of the Achaean League by the Romans in 146. In Rhodes, which was never humiliated by the Romans, many inscriptions are still in more or less consistent dialect in the first century A.D.

So much for the evidence of inscriptions. It is a reasonable supposition that local dialects continued to be spoken in the countryside, albeit in an impure form, long after they had lost prestige among the urban upper classes and ceased to be used in inscriptions. The scanty evidence of contemporary writers supports the view that in some areas a form of speech recognisable as° Doric persisted into the second century A.D. Suetonius, *Tib.* 56, indicates that Doric of a sort was generally spoken in Rhodes in the early first century. Strabo (8.1.2) states that all the Peloponnesian communities spoke Doric at the end of the first century B.C. And Strabo is only interested in cities, not in the countryside. Dio Chrysostom (*c.* A.D. 40–A.D. 115) met an old woman in the Peloponnese who addressed him in Doric, about A.D. 100. And Pausanias (4.27.11) tells us that the Messenians in his day – the middle of the second century – still preserved their dialect.

It seems likely, then, that in Old Greece, and particularly in the less accessible regions of the Peloponnese, dialect speech, or a form of Koine heavily coloured by dialect features, persisted for several centuries into the Christian era. This explains the Doric features found in certain modern Greek dialects, particularly the highly aberrant Tsakonian and South Italian dialects, which seem to have separated off from common Greek some time in the dark ages. Similar conditions in some parts of the interior of

Asia Minor may explain the phonetic developments found in the modern Asia Minor dialects. On these matters cf. pp. 127–8 below.

1. cf. Meillet (1935) 241 ff.; Thumb (1901); Debrunner (1954); Radermacher (1947); Costas (1936).

2. Humbert (1930) 21–25.

3. Black (1954).

4. On the language of the N.T. and its position in the spectrum of post-classical Greek cf. Moulton (1908); Tabachovitz (1956); Blass-Debrunner (1961); Rydbeck (1967).

5. Trubetzkoy (1939).

6. Worrell (1934); Till (1961).

7. cf. Chantraine (1927); Mihevc (1959). For false reduplications cf. ἐχρεώστηται (Malalas), ἐποιήκατε (Malalas), κεκτισμένος (Malalas), ῥερυπωμένην (Moschos). Frequent third persons plural perfect in -αν are a further indication of the confusion of perfect and aorist, e.g. πέπραχαν (Malalas): to these correspond the third persons plural aorist in -ασι, such as διεθήκασι (Moschos).

8. The recent controversy regarding the place of the optative in literary Greek of the period, which some scholars believed to reflect the usage of contemporary spoken Greek, has now largely died down. The optative of literary Greek in this period was maintained in use by literary and grammatical tradition, not by living usage: hence its uncertainty and imprecision. Most of the literature, and all the valid arguments, regarding this controversy, will be found in Henry (1943), Higgins (1945) and Anlauf (1960).

9. Throughout late Koine and medieval Greek a number of rival patterns for the expression of futurity coexist. It is not until the modern period that a single future pattern, capable of expressing the two aspects of the Greek verb, emerges (demotic θὰ + subjunctive and corresponding forms in the dialects, e.g. ἐννὰ + subjunctive). In some dialects of Asia Minor there is still a structural imbalance, in so far as distinctions of aspect are not expressed in the future. On the disappearance of the ancient future and its replacements in Koine, medieval and modern Greek cf. Bănescu (1915); Mirambel (1966) 187–188; Pernot (1946).

10. On the periphrasis with εἰμί and the present participle cf. Björck (1940): on this and other periphrastic verbal forms with εἰμί and ἔχω in ancient, medieval and modern Greek cf. Aerts (1965).

11. On this very frequent periphrasis in late Koine and early medieval Greek cf. Dieterich (1898) 246; Jannaris (1897) 553–555; Chatzidakis (1905) I, 602; Psaltes (1913) 216–217; Mihevc-Gabrovec (1960). The earliest examples seem to belong to the sixth century A.D.

12. On the disappearance of the dative and its substitutes cf. Humbert (1930); Mihevc-Gabrovec (1960) 20–24; Jannaris (1897) 341–347.

13. On productive and unproductive suffixes in Koine cf. Palmer (1945) 6–18.

14. On Latin loan-words cf. Viscidi (1944); Triantaphyllides (1909); Magie (1905); Cameron (1931); Zilliacus (1935).

15. The lists of words in Buck and Petersen (1939) are revealing of the freedom with which vocabulary was extended in this period, though many of the statements regarding the first attestation of a word are in need of revision.

16. Indeed many sub-literary texts make a very extensive but rather slap-dash use of the infinitive, which, though it was losing its place in the system of the language, was available to speakers for a variety of purposes. In particular the substantival infinitive used with the article provides an alternative for various types of subordinate clause which speakers and writers were no longer sure of forming correctly and unambiguously. cf. Weierholt (1963) 38–53.

17. Trypanis (1960).

18. On this consecutive or final use of καί cf. Ljungvik (1932) 39–64; Tabachovitz (1943) 8–10.

19. On the language and style of Greek prose writers influenced by the Atticist movement, the standard work is still Schmid (1887–1897) rpt. 1966; cf. also Triantaphyllides (1937).

20. Galen VI 633.4 K.

21. Galen XIV 624.17 K.

22. Galen VIII 581–588 K.

23. M. Aurelius ap. Fronto *ep.* p. 22.16–20 van den Hout.

24. cf. Ljungvik (1926); Ghedini (1937).

25. Fabricius (1962), (1967).

26. cf. Wahrmann (1907); Debrunner (1954) 34–69.

THE GREEK LANGUAGE IN THE EARLY

MIDDLE AGES (6TH CENTURY–1100)

In 634 the city of Bostra, capital of the province of Arabia, fell to the Arabs under Omar. Cities on the desert fringe had been raided before. But this was no raid. A great Byzantine army was defeated on the river Yarmuk in Palestine on 20 August 636, which put the whole of Syria at the mercy of the Arabs. Damascus fell in the same year, and by 638 Antioch and Jerusalem were both captured. In 639 Byzantine Mesopotamia fell to the invaders. In 641 began the invasion of Egypt, the granary of the empire, and Alexandria fell in 646. In the meantime the Arabs had already occupied Cyrenaica and Tripolitania, and were thrusting deep into Asia Minor. Caesarea in Cappadocia fell to the Caliph Moawiya in 647. By 654 the Arabs possessed a fleet capable of conducting a devastating raid on Rhodes. In spite of some successful resistance by Constans II (641–668) and Constantine IV (668–685), and a peace treaty between Arabs and Byzantines in 659, Arab pressure continued. Annual Arab expeditions into Asia Minor recommenced in 663, and often penetrated as far as Chalkedon, on the Asiatic shore opposite Constantinople. Meanwhile their fleet attacked and occupied Rhodes, Cos and Chios, and established in Cyprus a kind of balance of terror with the Byzantines, as a result of which the population abandoned the cities and crossed over to the mainland or took to the hills. In 670 Cyzicus, in the Sea of Marmora, was taken, and in 672 Smyrna fell. In 674 the Arab fleet appeared under the walls of

Constantinople, linked up with the army which had marched across Asia Minor, and began a siege which was not raised until 678.

At the same time there were great losses of territory and movements of population in the north and west of the Byzantine empire. In 568 the Lombards burst into Italy, and within a few years only the extreme south of the peninsula and the region surrounding Ravenna were left in Byzantine hands. In 585 the Byzantine province of Spain was recaptured by the Visigoths. Slavonic peoples in alliance with the Avars from north of the Danube began pressing south into the Balkan peninsula about the middle of the sixth century. By about 580 they were settling in Moesia (present-day Bulgaria) and laying waste great areas of Greece, and a year or two later they began to settle in large numbers there too. Thessalonica was besieged for the first time in 584. By the later 580s the Slavs were in the Peloponnese. A mosaic of little Slavonic principalities covered a large part of the Balkan peninsula, and Byzantine control was limited to a number of coastal cities and strong points, and to the sea: though even there they could not prevent Slavonic expeditions against the Cyclades, Crete, and Southern Italy in the early seventh century. By the 60s of the century a new power, the Bulgars, appeared upon the Balkan scene, and succeeded in unifying under their rule the Slavonic settlers in the region north of Greece. In 681 the Byzantines were forced to conclude a humiliating peace.

During this period of struggle for existence, which continued until the second half of the eighth century, there were many movements of population, our knowledge of which is limited and scanty.[1] Sweeping administrative changes put an end to the separation of civil and military power and to the autonomy of the cities: in any case many cities sank to the level of agricultural villages. Schools were fewer, the level of education lower. In the eighth century the Iconoclast movement divided the empire on a theological issue which had important political and social overtones. This was in a period during which we might expect far-reaching changes to take place in the Greek language. Unfortunately, we have scarcely any direct evidence. Papyri in Greek become less common in the seventh century, and by the middle of the eighth they peter out: in any case the mass of the rural population of Egypt had never been Greek-speaking, or at any rate had not spoken Greek as its first language. Inscriptions are few and far between, and such as exist are jejune epitaphs containing little but proper names: to this there is one important group of exceptions (see below). Little literature was produced during the 'Dark Age' of the seventh and eighth centuries, and less has survived. We are very much worse placed to trace the evolution of the Greek language than during the period of the Roman empire. It is for this reason, among others, that the period of political breakdown and demographic change is not considered on its own, but as a part of a longer period, during the second half of which we are better off for evidence. But it must be remembered that many of the changes which are first attested in the second half of the period probably occurred during its turbulent first half.

Our knowledge of Greek during the period 600–1100 depends almost entirely upon literary texts. Those composed in the purist literary language tell us nothing that we wish to know, except in so far as occasionally they embody a quotation of informal, living speech. There are however, as there were in the previous period, a certain number of sub-literary texts representing an uneasy balance between the purist ideal and the speech of the people. These include chronicles: the *Paschal Chronicle*, composed shortly after 628, the *Chronography* of Theophanes, composed between 810 and 814, the *Breviarium* of the Patriarch Nicephorus of about the same date, the *Chronicle* of George the Monk, written about 867; saints' lives and other religious texts, such as the *Life of St John the Almsgiver* by Leontios of Neapolis, the *Life of St Philaretos*, the *Doctrina Iacobi nuper baptizati*; certain of the works of the emperor Constantine VII Porphyrogenitus (912–959) which are written in 'vulgar' language. In the period under review there is as yet no poetry in the language of the people, or at any rate none was thought worthy of being copied and preserved. But we do have the texts of some of the rhythmical acclamations with which the people greeted – not always in the friendliest of tones – the emperor on formal occasions, in particular in the Hippodrome: these are couched in the spoken tongue.[2] Little in the way of grammatical literature survives, and such as does survive does not as a rule refer to the spoken language. An important group of inscriptions are the so-called Protobulgarian Inscriptions. These are inscriptions in Greek set up in their territory by the Khans of Bulgaria or by other dignitaries of the Bulgarian state. Though written in Greek – the Turkic language of the Bulgars was never reduced to writing and the language of their Slavonic subjects, with whom they in

course of time merged, had to wait until the mid-ninth century
for an alphabet – these inscriptions are composed by men who
had little or no contact with the literary tradition, and who wrote
more or less as they spoke. Like all documents produced by the
semi-literate, they have to be used with the utmost caution. Yet
they are a valuable testimony to spoken Greek of their time.[3]

Some light is thrown upon the phonology and morphology
of spoken Greek by the many loan-words in other languages,
such as Arabic, Syriac, Latin, Old Slavonic, Armenian, Georgian,
medieval Hebrew, and the less numerous loan-words from these
languages in Greek. For instance the Slavonic proper name
Čurila from Κύριλλος confirms the hypothesis, made on other
grounds, that as late as the ninth century upsilon was still ü
and had not become i. But in the main these loan-words throw
light on the development of the borrowing languages rather than
on that of Greek.

In the sphere of phonology there was little change from the
end of the previous period. The six-vowel system, with ü, was
simplified to a triangular five-vowel system

when ü became i. This pronunciation probably began in the late
Roman empire. But as late as the tenth century it was still possible to make fun of an ecclesiastical dignitary by suggesting that
he confused the two vowels. The implication is that the confusion
was, in Constantinople at any rate, a mark of vulgar speech,
whereas men of education still strove to keep the vowels distinct, much as in France today it is only by a conscious effort
that men of education keep distinct the nasalised vowels of *brun*
and *brin*, confused in the speech of the common people. Two
developments in the pronunciation of consonants, which occur
frequently but sporadically in papyri from Egypt, became general
in the period under review, and are reflected in literary texts.
The first is the simplification of double consonants, the second
the omission of final -*v* except before a following vowel. Some of
the dialects of modern Greek preserve double consonants and
final -*v*. So the change, radiating from an influential centre, perhaps Constantinople, never spread over the whole Greek-speaking
world, and only its beginnings fall within this period.

At some time in the early middle ages a phonological change took place, many of whose effects were masked by analogical influences. Pretonic initial vowels disappeared. Thus:

ὀσπήτιον	>	σπίτι 'house'
ἡμέρα	>	μέρα 'day'
οὐδέν	>	δέν 'not'
ἐρωτῶ	>	ρωτῶ 'ask'
ὀλίγος	>	λίγος 'little'
εὑρίσκω	>	βρίσκω 'find'
ὑψηλός	>	ψηλός 'high'
ὀψάριον	>	ψάρι 'fish'
ὡσάν	>	σάν 'as' etc.

These were probably at first allegro-forms, characteristic of rapid or informal speech, and coexisted with the full forms. The analogy of forms in which the initial vowel was accented, and above all the influence of the learned language, caused the vowel to be restored in a great many cases. Thus ἐλευθερία 'freedom' exists today side by side with λευτεριά, and Ἑλλάδα 'Greece' keeps its initial vowel under the influence of Ἕλληνας 'Greek'. Among the effects of this aphaeresis of pretonic initial vowels are:

(1) The development of the enclitic third person pronouns τον, την, το, του, της, τους, τας, των from αὐτόν, αὐτήν etc. In origin these forms have nothing to do with the definite article.

(2) The disappearance of the temporal augment, except when accented. Thus we have ἔφερα, ἔδωσα, but φέρθηκα, δώθηκα. In some dialects it has been restored analogically.

(3) The development of the demotic forms στόν στήν, στό, στούς etc. from εἰς τόν, εἰς τήν etc.

(4) The development of certain new demotic verbal prefixes. Thus ἐξυπνῶ > ξυπνῶ 'waken', ἐξέλαβα > ξέλαβα 'tooth out', ἐξέκοψα > ξέκοψα 'cut out', whence ξεκόβω. From such forms as these the new verbal prefix ξε- was abstracted. Similarly the compound prefix ἐξανα- > ξανα-. ἐμβαίνω > μπαίνω 'enter', ἐκδύνω > γδύνω 'undress'.

This process of aphaeresis is found in all Greek dialects today, including those of southern Italy, where we have kúo (ἀκούω 'hear'), gro (ὑγρός 'wet'), koδespina (οἰκοδέσποινα 'mistress of

the house'), *stéo* (ὀστέον 'bone') etc. But in none did it proceed
unhindered by the influences of analogy and of the purist tongue.

In the domain of morphology a number of changes can be
traced, though none can be dated with precision. In any case
dates are meaningless in such matters, since old and new patterns
coexist for a long time in the speech habits of a community. In
the noun, the dative case forms passed out of living use finally,
surviving only in lexicalised clichés such as δόξα τῷ Θεῷ 'thank
God'. Any written text will still contain datives, although alternative forms of expression were available for every usage of the
dative. A wide-ranging rearrangement of noun paradigms took
place, in which the distinction between vocalic and consonantal
stems, still in full force in late koine Greek, was surmounted.
A complex interplay of analogies was involved, but the course
of events can be summarised thus: vowel-stem substantives,
which were very numerous now made use of the distinction -ς,
-ν, -ο in the singular: masculines had nominative in -ς,
accusative in -ν, and genitive in -ο, e.g. λόγο-ς, λόγο-ν, λόγου,
ναύτης, ναύτην, ναύτη 'sailor'. Feminines had nominative in -ο,
accusative in -ν, and genitive in -ς, e.g. νύμφη, νύμφην, νύμφης,
'bride', χώρα, χώραν, χώρας 'land'. Side by side with these
there existed a number of consonantal stems with a different
pattern, e.g. πατήρ, πατέρα, πατρός 'father', μήτηρ, μητέρα,
μητρός 'mother', φύλαξ, φύλακα, φύλακος 'guard', Ἑλλάς,
Ἑλλάδα, Ἑλλάδος 'Greece'. Since the common feature of all
the vowel-stem nouns was that their accusative singular ended in
-ν, -ν was added to the accusative singular of the consonant-
stem nouns, giving the forms πατέραν, μητέραν, φύλακαν,
Ἑλλάδαν. Around this new accusative singular a new paradigm
was constructed after the model of the vowel-stem nouns, thus
from acc. πατέραν was formed nom. πατέρας and gen. πατέρα,
from acc. μητέραν was formed nom. μητέρα and gen. μητέρας;
similarly the paradigms φύλακας, φύλακαν, φύλακα, and
Ἑλλάδα, Ἑλλάδαν, Ἑλλάδας were formed. This new pattern
enabled the singular forms of the vast majority of Greek masculine and feminine nouns to be formed in accordance with two
simple paradigms. Neuter substantives still followed a series of
patterns of their own, with only two forms. Incidentally one of
the effects of the new rearrangement of substantives was to iso-
late feminines in -ος. Many of them simply became masculine.

Thus we find ὁ βάτος 'bush', ὁ πλάτανος 'plane-tree', ὁ ψῆφος 'pebble, vote', ὁ ἄμμος 'sand' etc. Others were replaced by feminine forms in -η or -α, thus ἡ ἀσβόλη 'soot' ἡ Σύρα, occasionally ἡ παρθένα, ἡ παρθένη 'maiden'. A few formed a rather labile group of feminines in -ο or -ον, e.g. we find ἡ ἄμμο etc. The plural of substantives presented different problems. It did not necessarily mark gender, as did the singular. And the consonant stem nominative ending had from the κοινή period been invading the masculine and feminine a-stems. Thus χῶρες replaced χῶραι, ναῦτες replaced ναῦται. The reason is firstly phonetic, resulting from the monophthongisation of αι to ε, and secondly structural: the parallelism of χῶραι (pronounced χῶρε): χώρας and μητέρες; μητέρας led to the substitution of χῶρες for χῶραι. Thus a-stem nouns and consonant stem nouns agreed in the paradigm -ες, -ας, -ων (-ῶν) in the plural. Only the o-stem nouns maintained a distinct paradigm in -οι, -ους, -ων. At the same time the loss of the sense of distinction between nouns with a vocalic and those with a consonantal stem led to the extension of certain consonant stem plural endings to other consonant stems and to vowel stems. In particular the endings -άδες, -άδας, -άδων and -ιδες, -ιδας, -ίδων abstracted from substantives such as φυγάς, φυγάδες 'exile'; δακτυλίς, δακτυλίδες 'ring' became extended to a greater variety of other substantives, replacing the plural endings -ες, -ας, -ων. Parisyllabic and imparisyllabic plurals often exist side by side. Only masculine o- stems never have imparisyllabic plurals. e- stems and u- stems always have them in modern Greek, and probably this characteristic dates from the rearrangement of noun paradigms in the early middle ages. One of the advantages of the imparisyllabic pattern was that it preserved the vowel of the singular stem, which would otherwise have vanished in the plural, since plurals – other than those of o- stems – were now formed with consonantal stems and vocalic terminations, πατέρ-ες, πατέρ-ας, πατέρ-ων as opposed to singular πατέρα-ς, -ν, -ο. This no doubt explains why καφέδες 'coffee' and παππούδες 'grandfather' are the only plural forms found today from καφές and παππούς; it would otherwise have been impossible to preserve the distinctive vowels in the plural. A result of this remodelling of the nominal declensions is that – o- stems apart – singular and plural of a Greek noun no longer had the same stem, and hence there was no necessary one-to-one correlation between them.[4]

In the definite article there is probably one morphological

3

change which must be attributed to the period under discussion,
although it is not directly attested during this period. Sporadic
examples occur, however, in earlier papyri, and when in the
twelfth century we once again have extensive demotic texts we
find it completed. It is the substitution of οἱ for αἱ in the nominative plural feminine. It is probably to be explained by the
analogy of the plural forms of nouns which were largely common
to masculine and feminine. It is interesting that in the Greek of
Bova in Calabria the originally feminine form αἱ has been extended to the masculine article. The replacement of the form τάς
by τές in the acc.pl.fem. may have taken place in this period.
But it is part of a general process, the extension of -ες to the
accusative pl. of all masc. and fem. nouns other than o- stems,
which was not completed until the subsequent period. The dative
forms of the article, singular and plural, naturally passed out of
living use with the disappearance of the dative case as a morphological and syntactical category.

The series of demonstrative pronouns was slightly remodelled.
ὅδε is rare in vulgar Koine texts – in the New Testament it hardly
occurs except in the form τάδε- and passed out of use in the
period under review. Its place was taken by αὐτός, which ceased
to be used in the meaning 'self', being replaced by ἴδιος. οὗτος
remained in use, but its paradigm was simplified, the stem τοῦτ-
being used throughout, giving τοῦτος, τούτη, τοῦτο etc. ἐκεῖνος
remained in use, though less frequent than in earlier periods. On
the analogy of ἐκεῖνος we sometimes find ἐτοῦτος.

The relative pronoun was in a state of uncertainty, and viable
new forms were not established until the following period. ὅς,
ἥ, ὅ is still found, but is more often replaced by one of the
following:

(1) ὅστις, ἥτις, ὅτι, originally an indefinite relative pronoun,
'whoever'; but the confusion begins in classical times.

(2) τίς, τί. The use of interrogative pronouns as relatives is
common in many languages.

(3) τόν, τήν, τό etc. This is very common in the accusative
and genitive; cases of ὁ, ἡ, τό in the nominative are rare. Examples of this use of forms, identical with those of the definite
article, appear in early Hellenistic times, and are common in the
later Koine, e.g. τὰ βουΐδια τὰ ἐλάβατε 'the oxen which we got',
εἰς τὸν τόπον τὸν ὁ Θεὸς σὲ ἔδωκεν 'in the place which God gave
you', ἐκεῖνο τὸ ἐφάγαμεν 'that which we ate'. In the period

under review it was the commonest form of the relative pronoun, and remained in living use until the sixteenth century, though to an ever growing extent replaced by ὅπου, ὁποῦ, ποῦ and ὁποῖος.

The system of the personal pronouns was extensively remodelled, though it is very difficult to reconstruct the details of the process. Side by side with the emphatic forms ἐμέ, ἐμοῦ, new forms ἐσέ, ἐσοῦ were created by analogy. A new second person plural ἐσεῖς, ἐσᾶς, ἐσῶν was created on the analogy of ἐσέ etc. and is first attested in the seventh century. In due course ἡμεῖς and ὑμεῖς became homophonous, but ὑμεῖς had already been replaced in spoken Greek by the new forms before this occurred. After the period under review this process of remodelling was completed by the replacement of ἡμεῖς, ἡμᾶς, ἡμῶν by ἐμεῖς, ἐμᾶς, ἐμῶν on the analogy of the singular. At the same time the principle of distinction between emphatic forms with a vocalic prefix and enclitic forms without it was carried through, resulting in the following paradigm in the first and second persons:

ἐγώ	ἡμεῖς, ἐμεῖς
ἐμέ μέ	ἡμᾶς, ἐμᾶς, μᾶς
ἐμοῦ μου	ἡμῶν, ἐμῶν (μῶν)
ἐσύ	ἐσεῖς σεῖς
ἐσέ σε	ἐσᾶς σᾶς
ἐσοῦ σου	ἐσῶν (σῶν)

The forms in brackets are rare or doubtful; the enclitic form of the accusative seems even at this period to have been used for the genitive. The third person pronoun αὐτός, originally an anaphoric pronoun, was drawn into the system of the personal pronouns, and provided with similar enclitic forms, thus:

αὐτός	αὐτή	αὐτό
αὐτόν τον	αὐτήν την	αὐτό το
αὐτοῦ του	αὐτῆς της	αὐτοῦ του
αὐτοί	αὐτές	αὐτά
αὐτούς τους	αὐτάς τας	αὐτά τα
αὐτῶν των	αὐτῶν των	αὐτῶν των

A further change, the details of which are even less clear, affected the emphatic forms of the first and second persons singular. ἐμέ and ἐσέ acquired a final -ν, presumably on the analogy of demonstrative and other pronouns. (ἐ)σέν first appears in the second century and ἐμέν in the third, but they remain rare in Koine Greek.

The next step was to 'normalise' the accusative forms ἐμέν and ἐσέν, which are isolated, by treating them as consonantal noun stems, and attaching the accusative termination -αν to them, giving ἐμέναν and ἐσέναν. ἐμέναν is first attested in the fourth century; and when in the twelfth century demotic texts are once again available, ἐμέναν and ἐσέναν are the regular emphatic forms. So the change outlined above presumably took place during the period under discussion.[5]

In the domain of the verb the non-personal forms, infinitive and participle remained in use throughout the period under review; in the chronicles infinitives were used in final-consecutive sense, as object of a great variety of verbs, and, as substantives with the article, while participles were in the main used circumstantially. Both are very frequent in the *Chronography* of Theophanes, who can write such a sentence as γνόντες δὲ οἱ 'Ρωμαῖοι τὴν ἔφοδον τοῦ Σαρβαραζᾶ εἰς δειλίαν ἐτράπησαν, καί τοῖς ποσὶ τοῦ βασιλέως προσέπεσον δάκρυσι μετανοοῦντες διὰ τὴν κακῶς γενομένην αὐτῶν παρακοήν, γνόντες οἷον κακῶν ἐστι δούλων μὴ εἰκεῖν τοῖς τοῦ δεσπότου βουλεύμασι 'The Romans, learning of the approach of Sarbarazas, turned craven, and fell at the feet of the emperor in tears, repenting of their ill-conceived disobedience, knowing that it is the mark of bad servants not to give way to the designs of their master.' This is far from spoken Greek; and each of the participles and infinitives (set spaced) in this passage could readily be replaced by a construction with a finite verb form γνόντες → ὅταν ἔγνωσαν, μετανοοῦντες → καί μετενόησαν, γενομένην → ἥτις ἐγένετο, γνόντες → διότι ἔγνωσαν, εἰκεῖν → ἵνα εἴκουσι.

So both infinitive and participle were by this time, if not earlier, in process of desystematisation. The infinitive certainly survived in living, though restricted, use after the end of the period, and indeed still survives in a fossilised form in certain modern Greek periphrastic forms. The position of the participle was already much weakened. The majority of participles, even in Theophanes' *Chronographia*, are circumstantial participles, adverbial in function, playing exactly the same role in the sentence as the modern Greek indeclinable gerund in -οντας which is the continuation of the earlier active participles. Moreover we find frequent confusion between tenses of the active participle, between genders, and between cases, e.g. τὸν ἀναπληροῦντα τὸν τόπον τὸν ἐμόν 'the man who will take my place' (=future) Theoph.; πλήθη συρρευσάντων δυνάμεων 'a number of powers coalescing' Theophyl; πάντων γυναικῶν 'of all women', Acta Thomae; τό παιδίον ζῶντα 'the child alive', Vct. Epiph.; ἡ ψυχὴ βοᾷ λέγοντα 'the soul cries out saying', Apoc. Mar.; τά ῥηθέν, τῶν δοθέν, etc. We also find participles used in coordination with finite verbs, e.g. δεξάμενος οὖν ὁ βασιλεὺς τὰ γράμματα παρὰ 'Επιφανίου καὶ ἐποίησεν τύπον τοιοῦτον 'So the emperor, receiving the letter of Epiphanios, and made the following order'. By the end of the period under review we begin to find an indeclinable form in -οντα used either adverbially or predicatively, e.g. ἡμεῖς βλέποντα (a document from southern Italy dated 999), ἐὰν φανῶμεν καταζητοῦντα καὶ ἐνοχλοῦντα (a document of 1034). But the Prodromic poems still use declined active participles. The passive participles in -όμενος and -μένος, on the other hand, remain in undiminished use, and fully inflected.⁶

Correspondingly the verbal periphrases involving an active participle listed in the previous chapter become less frequent, while the periphrases with the infinitive remain in use. The commonest future periphrasis is that with ἔχω + infinitive; but the commonest expression of futurity is probably the present indicative.

The vestiges of the perfect active become fused with the aorist, giving rise to the frequent aorists in -κα found in all dialects of modern Greek. At the same time the periphrastic perfect active ἔχω + perfect participle passive, and its passive equivalent εἰμί + perfect participle passive, become firmly established. The verb in spoken Greek has by now in principle two themes, which express opposing aspects (continuous and momentary actions) in all moods, and which in the indicative only carry an additional distinction of time. There is uncertainty in the use of the syllabic augment, and we find such forms as παρείσφερεν, ἐπιδείκνυτο, ἐπισκόπησεν. This is connected with the tendency to eliminate pre-tonic initial vowels (p. 63). But the rule of Modern Common Demotic by which the augment is only retained when accented is a much later development. Modern Greek dialects vary very much in their treatment of the syllabic augment. The temporal augment is generally dropped, the initial vowel remaining unchanged. Occasional temporal augments of the first vowel of compound verbs, e.g. ἠπαίτησε, ἠφόρησε, are indications of the failure to analyse the compound verb correctly.

Of the various present-theme suffixes inherited by Greek only

a few remain productive. Apart from those used to form denominative verbs, -ίζω, -άζω, -εύω, one other purely verbal
suffix spreads in this period – -νω. We find such forms as δένω
for δέω, φέρνω for φέρω, χύνω for χέω. Along with the inherited
verbs in -νω and in -άνω or -αίνω these form a substantial group,
as a result of which a suffixed -ν- comes to be one of the main
marks of a present stem. It begins even to be extended to the
verbs with final accent (the old contract verbs); we find such
forms as κερνῶ 'mix' (κεράω), περνῶ 'cross over' (περάω) in
this period, forerunners of a large class of verbs in later spoken
Greek. Verbs in -όω tend to be reformed in -ώνω. In general,
the suffix -νω is used to form new present themes from aorist
themes.

The verb εἰμί 'to be' completes a development begun in the
previous period, the chief features of which are:

(1) The substitution of medio-passive endings for the anomalous athematic active endings. This perhaps began in the imperfect.

(2) The extension of the stem-vowel εἰ- to all persons and
numbers.

(3) The replacement of the third person present indicative
singular and plural forms by ἔνι (=ἔνεστι 'there exists').

The result of these processes is the establishment in the period
under review of the paradigm:[7]

εἰμαι	εἰμεθα	ἤμην	ἤμεθα
εἰσαι	(εἰσθε?)	ἦσο	?
ἔνι	ἔνι	ἦτο(ν)	ἦσαν, ἦν, ἦταν

The scarcity of texts reflecting the spoken language makes it
difficult to say much about the development of the vocabulary.
Most of the suffixes productive in the previous period continue
to be productive. -ᾶς begins to replace -άριος as an agent suffix,
but does not completely replace it. Verbal abstracts in -σιμο(ν)
occur more frequently – the earliest, isolated, example occurs in
a papyrus of fifth or sixth century. There is also an extension of
verbal nouns in -μα. There is a considerable extension of the
feminine suffix -ισσα, resulting from the remodelling of the noun-
paradigm, which henceforth excluded feminine substantives in
-ος. Neuter diminutives in -ιον, -άριον, -άδιον, -ίδιον, -άκιον,

-ίκιον become more numerous. The new suffix -τζι(ν), -ίτζι(ν) makes its appearance, mainly in personal names, but also in such common nouns as ἡνίτζιν 'bridle', σικιπινίτζιν (?), σταυρίτζιν 'cross', προαστίτζιν 'farm'; its origin is disputed, some authorities believing it to be due to Slavonic influence, others to palatalisation of -ίκιο(ν). There are a few instances in the period under review of the suffix -πουλον, e.g. ἀρμενόπουλον, ἀρχοντόπουλον, ἀββαδόπουλον, and of its masculine counterpart -πουλος, e.g. Ἀργυρόπουλος, Γαβριηλόπουλος, Δουλόπουλος (sic.), Σθλαβόπουλος.[8] The adjectival suffix -ᾶτος, of Latin origin, is highly productive, even with Greek stems, c.g. ἱκανᾶτος, κωδωνᾶτος, as is also the originally Latin -ιανός. -εύω, -ίζω, -άζω, -όω (-ώνω) remain the only productive verbal suffixes.

As in earlier and later Greek, composition remains a fertile source of new vocabulary. Copulative compounds, which are rare in classical and Koine Greek, become frequent in the period under review, e.g. ἀριστόδειπνον 'lunch and dinner', εἰσοδο-έξοδος 'entry and exit', ὑποκαμισοβράκιον 'shirt and trousers', ἀνδρόγυνος 'man and wife',[9] τοξοφάρετρον 'bow and quiver', πρασινοβένετος 'green and blue'. Determinative compounds whose second member is a substantive (Karmadharaya compounds) are extremely numerous, as are also compound verbal adjectives in -τος, the first element of which stands in casual relation to the second (Tatpurusa compounds), e.g. Θεόβλαστος 'sprung from God', χρυσοστοίβαστος 'heaped with gold'. Verbal compounds are found in which the first element is not a preposition, e.g. τοποτηρέω 'represent', μηροκλάζω 'break leg', σιδηροδέω 'fetter', ἀσπροφορέω 'wear white', ὀφθαλμοπλανέω 'have a roving eye'. Compound verbs formed from a compound noun and adjective whose second element is verbal are of course common, as they were in earlier periods of the language.

Latin continues to be the chief source of loan-words. But as the court and the upper strata of society ceased to be even theoretically bilingual, the number of new Latin loan-words belonging to the sphere of administration diminished. Such Latin loan-words as do occur for the first time in the period under review occasionally show signs of originating in the spoken Latin of the Balkan provinces, rather than in the literary Latin of lawyers and administrators. An example is πε(ν)τζιμέντον 'baggage' (from impedimentum), which shows the Balkan Latin substitution of affricate for dental plosive before a front vowel.[10] It is rarely possible during this period to distinguish Italian loan-words from Latin loan-words, and in the earlier part of the period the distinction is meaningless. Though there are no certain Italian loan-words in texts of the period, it seems likely that the flow of Italian words, particularly concerning maritime life, trade, etc. which is so striking in the following period, began in that at present under discussion. Arabic and Persian borrowings mostly concern features of oriental life, titles, etc., e.g. ἀμερουμνής, ἀμιρᾶς, μασγίδιον. But there are a few loan-words belonging to other spheres, e.g. τζιτζάκιον (possibly Chazar), ζιγγίβερ, τζάγγιον, τζουκανιστήριον (Greek derivative of Persian loan-word), βατάν, ζάβα. The first Slavonic loan-words make their appearance in this period. All are titles, e.g. βοϊλᾶς, βοάνος, χαγάνος.

1. Charanis (1959).

2. Maas (1912).

3. The latest and best edition is by Beševliev (1966) in which the editor discusses at length the evidence which they afford for the Greek language, and gives an exhaustive bibliography of earlier works. There is a good popular account of them in the English language periodical *Obzor*, published in Sofia, no. 2 (1968).

4. On the remodelling of the noun paradigm cf., in addition to the material in Dieterich (1898) 149–174 and Jannaris (1897) 101–136, also Seiler (1958).

5. On the development of the personal pronouns cf., in addition to Dieterich (1898) 189–192 and Jannaris (1897) 347, the interesting but not always entirely convincing reconstruction of their history in the light of structural linguistics by Dressler (1966).

6. On the development of the participle cf. Mirambel (1961).

7. On the development of the medieval and modern Greek forms of the substantive verb cf. Pernot (1891), (1946) 252; Dieterich (1898) 223–228; Kapsomenos (1953).

8. Misinterpreted as the title of an office, 'slave-dealer', by Dölger (1952). This is an interesting example of the importance of modern Greek for the understanding of medieval Greek texts.

9. It is significant that this word means 'effeminate man' in classical Greek, from Herodotus onwards; i.e. it is a determinative, not a copulative compound. Plato's use of it in the *Symposium* to denote a hermaphrodite, half-man and half-woman, is isolated in classical texts.

10. Rosetti (1943) 72–74; Battisti (1950) 151; Mihăescu (1960) 93–95.

4

THE GREEK LANGUAGE IN THE
LATER MIDDLE AGES (1100–1453)

In the course of these centuries there occurred a number of developments in the history of the Greek-speaking people, which are reflected in the history of the language, and even profoundly affected it. Nevertheless, it must be made clear at the outset that they are all of secondary character. Modern Greek took its shape in the previous period, above all in its earlier half. The accident – from the linguistic point of view, though of course it is not an accident for the historian – that we have a great deal more evidence for the spoken language from the later middle ages than from the earlier middle ages attracted scholars to the later period. And misunderstanding of the nature of the mixed language in which the late medieval texts are in the main written often caused them to date the changes by which the Modern Greek language was formed to a period many centuries too late. This point has been discussed in Chapter 1.

At the end of the eleventh century the greater part of Asia Minor was conquered and occupied by the Seljuk Turks. Large areas in the west of the peninsula were regained by the Byzantines in the first half of the twelfth century. But their tenure was weak and uncertain. By the early thirteenth century Asia Minor was once again largely in Seljuk hands, or in those of the Turcoman subjects of the Seljuks. Only in the extreme west and north-west where the Nicaean empire controlled a fairly large and firmly administered territory, in the north-east, where the Empire of

Trebizond held the coast from Sinope to east of Trebizond and some of the valleys running south into the mountains of Pontus, and fought with the Turcomans for control of the high mountain pastures, and in the south-east, where the Armenian principality of Little Armenia controlled most of Cilicia, did substantial areas remain free from Turkish control. By the early fourteenth century the Turks, now under the leadership of the Ottoman emirs from Northwest Asia Minor, had driven the Byzantines out of the mainland of Asia Minor. Only the Pontic coast and the upland valleys behind it remained in Greek hands, under local Greek rulers. By the middle of the century the Ottoman Turks, invited by one side in a Byzantine dynastic war, had established themselves in the Balkan peninsula. By the end of the century all that remained as Byzantine territory was the capital itself, with a few square miles of land surrounding it, Thessalonica and its immediate hinterland, a few points on the north shore of the Sea of Marmara, and the greater part of the Peloponnese. In 1453 Constantinople itself was captured by the Turks, and a few years later the Peloponnese and the empire of Trebizond had fallen to them. The common characteristics which most of the Greek dialects of Asia Minor show as compared with those of the rest of the Greek world no doubt reflect this early isolation from metropolitan influences, and the closer and more intimate contact with Turkish speakers which the Asia Minor Greeks had over the centuries. The influx of Turkish loan-words into Greek begins in the period under review.

Byzantium, too, was brought into close and not always friendly contact with western Europe, during this period. From the end of the eleventh century successive armies of Crusaders passed through Byzantine territory, and bodies of French, Italian, Spanish and German soldiers began to serve as mercenaries under the Byzantine High Command – a step rendered necessary largely by the loss of the man-power of Asia Minor. At the same time communities of western merchants and traders began to settle in Constantinople and in all the coastal cities of the Byzantine Empire. These included Amalfitans, Pisans, Neapolitans, Florentines and others, but above all colonists from Venice and Genoa. In a remarkably short time, and by means which have never properly been explained, they came to dominate Byzantine seaborne trade, and to drain off to the West the enormous gold reserves of the Empire. The Latin communities in Constantinople and many of the cities of the empire were prosperous and numerous. Byzantine ruling circles despised them for their lack of culture – while often concluding advantageous bargains with them for the sale of the produce of their estates. The mass of the people mistrusted them: relations were often tense, and there were occasional pogroms, as in 1182, when the Venetian community in Constantinople was massacred.

In 1204 came the diversion of the Fourth Crusade, the capture of Constantinople, and the establishment of the rickety Latin Empire. There was no longer a centralised Byzantine State. Greek successor states sprang up in Epirus, in north-west Asia Minor and in Pontus. The bulk of the western territories of the Empire passed into Latin hands, often never to leave them for centuries. Cyprus, captured by Richard Cœur-de-Lion in a fit of absence of mind, passed into the hands of the French Lusignans and their feudal barons. Crete became a Venetian possession, and remained one until the second half of the seventeenth century. Rhodes fell to the Knights of St John. The islands of the Cyclades were divided between Genoa, Venice, and a multiplicity of half-independent states set up by western adventurers. Euboea was Venetian, as were a number of strong-points round the Peloponnesian coast. The rest of the Peloponnese became the Principality of the Morea, ruled by the Villehardouin family, though later the Byzantines succeeded in regaining possession of the greater part of the peninsula. Attica, Boeotia and other parts of central Greece came under the Burgundian Lords of Athens, later Dukes of Athens – which is why Theseus is given this title by Dante, Boccaccio, Chaucer and Shakespeare. Further north was the ephemeral Kingdom of Thessalonica. Between these major states and in their interstices lay a number of tiny feudal Latin states, whose frontiers constantly changed, and which were fused or separated by the chances of war or dynastic marriage. The Ionian Islands were divided between Italian principalities, ruled mainly by the Tocco family, and Venetian domains.

The effects of the Latin conquest were complex. Latin loan-words flooded into the language: and in this context Latin refers not to the classical language of Rome, but to the Romance vernaculars spoken in the Mediterranean area. Italian loan-words are probably the most frequent. But they are often taken from peripheral dialects of Italian, in particular from Venetian. Next in frequency come French loan-words. And finally a thin scattering of borrowings from Provençal, Catalan, Spanish, etc. One would expect that these borrowed words first entered

Greek in areas controlled by speakers of the language from which
each was borrowed. But there is no direct evidence for this.
And we must remember that the Latin community of Outremer
was fairly polyglot. In fact it is easier to establish semantic fields
in which words were borrowed from particular languages. Thus
the vocabulary of feudal law and land-tenure is mainly French,
that of trade and seafaring mainly Italian.

But the Latin domination had more important effects. The
prestige of the literary language was lowered as the whole state
apparatus whose vehicle it had been was swept aside. The elaborate educational system which had maintained and inculcated
its use broke down. This does not mean that men at once began
to use the vernacular for literary purposes. Many of them still
sought to realise the old ideal of an unchanging written language.
Gregory of Cyprus who, unable to obtain a good Hellenic education in his native land under Lusignan rule, crossed Asia Minor
on foot in winter in order to pursue his education in Constantinople, now once again in Byzantine hands, is not an isolated
figure. In fact in the restored empire of the Palaiologoi there was
something of a literary renaissance in the old style, as part of
the attempt to recreate the old oecumenical Empire. But in the
great areas which remained permanently under Latin rule the
situation was different. Not only were they cut off from the cultural centre in Constantinople, not only was an education of the
old type more difficult to obtain, not only had they daily before
their eyes the example of their Latin rulers, who more and more
used the vernacular tongue for administrative and literary purposes, but a classical education was no longer the path to prefer-
ment. For we must not forget that one of the factors which gave
the literary language its prestige was that command of it could
lead to high positions in state and church. It was one of the paths
of social mobility in a highly stratified society. It is significant
that Gregory of Cyprus, of whom we have just spoken, in due
course became Oecumenical Patriarch. No doubt many other
lads who faced equal hardships in the pursuit of education never
rose high enough to leave a mark in history: but some careers
were open to certain kinds of talent. This was not so in Crete,
or Cyprus, or Attica, under Latin occupation.

Literature in something approaching the vernacular did not
begin only after the Latin conquest, nor was it confined to areas
under Latin rule. In the middle of the twelfth century Theodore
Prodromos and Michael Glykas wrote poems in the spoken

tongue as well as works in the purist literary language. And at least one of the semi-vernacular poems of chivalry, the tale of Kallimachos and Chrysorrhoe, was probably written by a prince of the imperial family in the early fourteenth century. But the new conditions created by the Latin conquests certainly furthered the break-through of the vernacular into literature.

Evidence for the spoken language is much more copious than in the preceding period. The epic poem of Digenis Akritas, which belongs to the tenth or eleventh century, is, in its surviving versions at any rate, composed in the literary tongue. One of the versions, that of the Escorial manuscript, shows many traits of the spoken tongue, however, and some scholars have thought that the poem was originally composed in the spoken language and later 'improved'. The poem *Spaneas* too is basically in the literary tongue, with sporadic concessions to spoken usage. The first substantial monuments of spoken Greek are the poems of Michael Glykas and the vernacular poems of Theodore Prodromos, both dating from the middle of the twelfth century. Glykas writes in a very uneven style. Passages of near-vernacular alternate with passages showing scarcely any vernacular features. The Prodromic poems, however, constitute a much more consistent attempt to reflect in literature the language of everyday speech of Constantinople. They are, like all the early vernacular poems, written in a mixed language. But the mixture contains a major proportion of living speech, recreated by a sensitive observer.

There is little vernacular writing that can be attributed to the thirteenth century, a time of turmoil in the Greek world. But about the year 1300 there was composed a long poetic chronicle, the *Chronicle of Morea*. There exist French, Italian and Aragonese versions of this chronicle, and some have held that it was originally composed in French and afterwards translated into Greek. At any rate the Greek version, whether original or translated, is the work of a man who had little or no contact with Byzantine tradition or with the literary tongue. He was probably a second or third generation French settler, Hellenised in language, but seeing the world through the eyes of the French of Outremer. This is a document of almost pure spoken Greek. But the word 'almost' is important. As was observed in Chapter 1, there are scattered words and phrases of the literary language, often used without understanding, like the classical nominative θυγάτηρ used as an accusative or genitive. And there are vernacular forms which today are in general not used in the same dialect, such as third persons plural of verbs in -ουν and -ουσι. Perhaps they were genuine alternatives in the language spoken by the writer. But it is more likely that he is using a mixed language, the result rather of lack of feeling for the language than of conscious effort to raise his style above that of everyday speech.

Finally we have a series of narrative poems, some of them adaptations – we must not speak of translations – from western exemplars, others wholly Greek in theme, though indebted in their manner to western influences in some degree. Some of them exist in several different versions, and it has been suggested that they may have been composed orally, and written down at different performances.

These poems include the romances of Lybistros and Rhodamne, Kallimachos and Chrysorrhoe, Belthandros and Chrysantza, Imberios and Margarona, and Phlorios and Platziaphlore, the story of Apollonios of Tyre, the Achilleid, the tale of Belisarios, several poems on the Trojan war, of which the longest – still unpublished – is an adaptation, direct or indirect, of the Old French poem of Benoît de Sainte-Maure, a version of the Alexander romance, several satirical poems of the *Animal Farm* type, the point of which is now lost for us, and various minor works. The only identifiable poet of the period is Leonardos Dellaportas, a Cretan in the Venetian service, who wrote a long dialogue between the poet and Truth, containing many autobiographical elements, as well as three shorter poems, about the beginning of the fifteenth century. An edition of these hitherto unknown poems by Professor M. I. Manoussakas is awaited.

None of these poems, apart from those of Dellaportas, the Alexander romance, and one of the animal poems, can be even approximately dated. Nor can they be attributed on linguistic grounds to any particular area of the Greek world. Either the modern dialects had not yet sufficiently differentiated – which seems unlikely – or there still existed, in spite of the political fragmentation of the Greek world, a common spoken language, at any rate among city dwellers. It is interesting to compare in this respect the poems of Dellaportas, which, in the excerpts so far published, show no typically Cretan dialect features, with the flourishing Cretan literature of the sixteenth and seventeenth centuries, which adopts a linguistic form based upon the living speech of Crete.

Prose literature in near-vernacular Greek is much less rich.

The Chronicle of Dukas, a few brief chronicles, the Cypriot
Chronicle of Leontios Makhairas, the Assizes of Cyprus, itself
a translation, and a number of unassuming paraphrases of works
composed in the literary language, virtually exhaust the list.[1]
Makhairas' Chronicle is composed in Cypriot vernacular, the
other works show no particular dialect features. There is also a
good deal of archival material from the period, some of which is
composed in the vernacular, and all of which is to some extent
influenced by it.

Changes in pronunciation no doubt took place during this
period. But with a few exceptions, to be discussed below, they
did not affect the phonological structure of the common language. The beginnings of the modern dialects are discernible;
though texts which show consistently the features of a particular
dialect are not found until later. Some of the dialects have a
phonological structure different from that of the common language, e.g. in respect of the treatment of unstressed vowels, or
of the palatalisation of -κ- to -č- before a front vowel. A phonological change in the common language which can be dated with
some probability to this period is the disappearance of final -ν,
except before a vowel or plosive in the following word, where the
two words form a single accentual group, e.g. article + substantive. Near vernacular texts of the twelfth century, such as the
Prodromic poems, generally preserve final -ν, but there is some
uncertainty. Thus we find $\beta\alpha\sigma\iota\lambda\acute{\epsilon}\alpha\nu$ and $\beta\alpha\sigma\iota\lambda\acute{\epsilon}\alpha$ 'King'. Frequently a final -ν appears where it has no historical justification,
e.g. $\theta\acute{\epsilon}\lambda\eta\mu\alpha$ 'will' but $\theta\acute{\epsilon}\lambda\eta\mu\acute{\alpha}\nu$ $\tau o\nu$, $\tau\grave{o}$ $\sigma\tau\acute{o}\mu\alpha\nu$ $\tau\eta s$ 'her mouth',
$\grave{\epsilon}\kappa\acute{o}\pi\eta\nu$ $\tau\grave{o}$ $\zeta\omega\nu\acute{\alpha}\rho\iota\nu$ $\mu o\upsilon$ 'my belt was cut'. By the fifteenth century
final -ν seems to have disappeared in the central areas of Greek
speech, except, as explained above, before a following vowel or
plosive. But in many dialects, e.g. those of Cyprus, of Crete, of
the Dodecanese, and of southern Italy, it still survives, and is
regularly added to certain forms in which it is not historically
justified.

It is probably in the course of this period that certain consonantal combinations involving plosive plus plosive, spirant plus
spirant, and σ plus spirant underwent a change in pronunciation,
the outcome of which, in most dialects, was as follows:

$$\left.\begin{array}{r}\kappa\tau \\ \chi\theta\end{array}\right\} > \chi\tau \qquad \left.\begin{array}{r}\pi\tau \\ \phi\theta\end{array}\right\} > \phi\tau \qquad \begin{array}{l}\sigma\theta > \sigma\tau \\ \sigma\chi > \sigma\kappa\end{array}$$

These changes are only sporadically attested in documents of the period. Even today, they are incomplete, in so far as loan-words from the purist language tend to preserve the traditional pronunciation. Ἐλευθερία is as common as, or even more common than, λευτεριά. Furthermore though -σθ- regularly becomes -στ-, the parallel change of -σχ- to -σκ- is only partially carried out: σχολεῖο is as good demotic as σκολειό, ἄσχημος as ἄσκημος. The change of σφ to σπ which might be expected does not occur. The Greek dialects of southern Italy have gone their own way in regard to these consonantal combinations. In Bova original πτ, φθ, κτ, χθ and σθ are all represented by st, e.g. está from ἑπτά, stíra 'louse' from φθείρα, ostró 'enemy' from ἐχθρός, epiástina from ἐπιάσθην etc. But in other villages of Calabria other patterns of assimilation are found, e.g. aléftora (ἀλέκτωρ), nítta, niθta (νύκτα), ettá, eθtá (ἑπτά). Apulian Greek develops ft from original κτ, χθ, e.g. nífta (νύκτα), ftinó (κτηνόν), from original πτ, φθ, e.g. ftoχó (πτωχός), eftá (ἑπτά), and from original σθ, e.g. afté (ἐχθές).[2]

A further change which took place in this period was the synizesis of ι and ε with a following vowel, accompanied by a shift of accent. Thus καρδία 'heart' became καρδιά, μηλέα 'apple-tree' became μηλιά, παλαιός 'old' became παλιός, παιδίου 'child's' became παιδιοῦ etc. This change did not take place simultaneously throughout the Greek world – indeed some dialects still preserve καρδία etc. – and we find in literary texts of the period forms with and without synizesis used side by side. Probably both forms long coexisted in living speech, the choice between them depending upon the tempo of utterance and the extra-linguistic situation.

The disappearance of final -ν had a drastic effect upon noun paradigms. As we have seen, the great majority of masculine and feminine substantives had been adapted to a single paradigm in the singular:

Masc. N.	-ας	Fem. N.	-α
Acc.	-αν	Acc.	-αν
Gen.	-α	Gen.	-ας

The loss of final -ν reduced the three forms of this paradigm to two:

Masc. N.	-ας	Fem. N.	}
Acc.	} -α	Acc.	} -α
Gen.	}	Gen.	-ας

Masculine o-stems still preserved three forms in the singular:

N.   -ος
Acc. -ο
Gen. -οι

A new class of neuters arose in -ι, with genitive in -ίου, becoming -ιοῦ by the same metathesis of accent which led to -ία becoming -ιά.

We thus have masculines in -ος, masculines in -ης, -ης (less frequently -ες, -ους), feminines in -α (-ία, -ιά), -η (plus a few in -ου, and proper names etc. in -ω), neuters in -ο and in -ι. Plurals of masculines and feminines are sometimes parisyllabic, sometimes imparisyllabic (-άδες, -ίδες etc.), the distribution of plural forms among the various singular forms being very uncertain. These patterns to which may be added that of neuters in -μα, Gen. -ματος, account for the vast majority of substantives in the living tongue. Certain inherited patterns other than these survive, e.g. neuters in -ος, Gen. -ους feminines in -ις, Gen. -εως but they are confined to a limited number of words and are not productive. An examination of 100 lines of the *Chronicle of the Morea* shows only the following substantives which do not follow one of the paradigms listed: τὸ πλῆθος 'mass', τοῦ πρίγκηπος 'prince' (a few lines earlier the normal nominative ὁ πρίγκιπας occurs), τὸ πλοῦτος 'wealth' (bis), τὸ μέρος 'place', τὰς χεῖρας 'hands'. By various analogical processes all adjectives were adapted to distinguish the three genders by separate forms. The inherited two-termination adjectives in -ος, -ον were given a feminine form in -η (-α): this is a process which was already at work in classical Greek, and had advanced considerably in the Koine. Adjectives in -ης, -ες were adapted in various ways; by metaplasis to -έος, -έα, -έον or -ος, -η, -ο, by creation of feminine stems in -α and neuter stems in -ικό, etc. Other adjectives with an originally consonantal stem were replaced by forms in -ος, -η, -ο; thus μέλανος appears for μέλας 'black' already in Koine, εὐσχήμων 'comely' is replaced by εὔσχημος etc. Adjectives in -ύς, -εῖα, -ύ, remain in living use, as they distinguish the three genders from the beginning. πᾶς, πᾶσα, πᾶν, though distinguishing the genders is replaced by ὅλος (cf. the replacement of *omnis* by *totus* in vulgar Latin). The fact that participles were no longer declined (see below) contributed to the disappearance of the consonant stem adjectives.

In the verb, distinctions of time are confined to the indicative. The two themes on which the verb is built serve in principle to distinguish aspect, and in subjunctive, imperative and infinitive (in so far as it survives) they distinguish only aspect. In part as a result of this, in part owing to the unsureness with which participial constructions were handled in Koine and early medieval Greek, the active participles are replaced by a single adverbial form in -οντα, later -οντας without any temporal content cf. *Belthandros and Chrysantza* 395 βλέποντα καὶ τὸ ζῴδιον θλιμμένα νὰ ἱστέκη 'seeing the beast standing dismayed', 1010 ἀκούοντα ὁ Βέλθανδρος οὐδὲν ἀπολογήθη 'Belthandros, hearing, made no defence', *Chronicle of the Morea*, Prol. 18 ἰδόντας τοῦθ' ὁ ἅγιος 'the saint seeing this', *Achilleis* 1464 βλέποντας τους ἀγούρους 'seeing the youths' (cf. 1343 ἰδόντας δὲ τὸ θέαμαν 'seeing the sight'): at this stage adverbial participles or gerundives in -οντας may be formed both from aorist and present themes, the distinction being one of aspect; in later Greek the formation is confined to the present stem. The loss of the old active participles appears to have taken place between the twelfth and fourteenth centuries. The poems of Theodore Prodromos use participles in accordance with classical rules, the *Chronicle of the Morea* shows complete failure to handle participial inflections; we find ἀκούσων ταῦτα (ἀκούσων being intended as an aorist participle), ἰδόντας γὰρ οἱ προεστοί, οἱ Φράγκοι . . . σφάζοντα, οἱ Φράγκοι . . . σκοτώνων, σκοπῶντα λογιζόμενος, διαβόντα ὁ καιρός, διαβὼν ὁ καιρός, λέγοντα καὶ ἀρνούμενος etc. But it may be that the change took place earlier in the Peloponnese than in Constantinople, or that Prodromos unwittingly introduces patterns from the literary language in his vernacular poems. Passive participles in -όμενος and -μένος continue to be declinable.[3]

We have seen that the formation of the future was in a state of flux. This condition continues during the period under review. The periphrasis with ἔχω + infinitive becomes less frequent. In part it is replaced by ἔχω νὰ + subjunctive, in the general process of the disappearance of the infinitive along with the other non-personal forms of the verb. But its principal replacements are periphrases with θέλω: θέλω + infinitive, θέλω νὰ + subjunctive, θὲ νὰ + subjunctive (earliest attested in the form θεννὰ in Cyprus in the twelfth century), θὰ νὰ + subjunctive. The forms θὲ and, by vowel assimilation θὰ, are presumably descended from the invariable θέλει, not from the personal θέλω, θέλεις etc.; the person is adequately indicated by the subjunctive forms. A similar invariable form from a verb meaning 'to wish' followed by a subjunctive marking the person occurs in other Balkan languages; the relation between these apparently parallel developments is far from clear.[4] However, in the period under discussion future periphrases with θέλω followed by infinitives were still in living use, though in general in other constructions the infinitive had been replaced by νά (ἵνα)+subjunctive.

One of the results of the development of a series of future periphrases with θέλω was to free the periphrasis consisting of ἔχω+infinitive (generally aorist) for other uses. In early medieval Greek, as we have seen, this was one of the future surrogates. Now if ἔχω ποιῆσαι can pass from the meaning 'I am able to do' to 'I shall do', εἶχα (εἶχον) ποιῆσαι can take on a conditional meaning 'I should or would do or have done'. This is actually found in late Koine and early medieval texts, e.g. Acta Philippi 58.15 εἰ δὲ καὶ σὺ τοιαῦτα πράγματα ἑώρακας (ἑώράκεις), οὐκ εἶχες ταραχθῆναι ἐπὶ τούτοις 'if you too had seen such things, would you not have been disturbed by them?' Malalas 128.5 εἶχον δὲ καὶ τὰς ἡμῶν ναῦς καῦσαι οἱ βάρβαροι, εἰ μὴ νὺξ ἐπῆλθε 'the barbarians would have burned our ships, had not night fallen'. Since the pluperfect indicative was also used as a conditional or past irrealis in late Koine, it was to be expected that εἶχα+aor. infin. would be used as a pluperfect, of anterior action in the past. The earliest certain examples are in texts of the period under review. In the *Chronicle of the Morea* we find

> ἔβαλαν τὸν βασιλέαν ἐκεῖνον
> εἰς τὸ σκαμνὶ τῆς βασιλείας ὅπου τὸ εἶχεν χάσει (622–3)

'they put that king on the royal throne which he had lost'

> κ' ηὖραν ἐκεῖ ὅτι εἶχε ἐλθεῖ ἐτότε ὁ Μέγας Κύρης
> ἐκ τὸ ῥηγάτο τῆς Φραγκίας, ὅπου τὸν εἶχεν στίλει
> ... ὁ πρίγκιπας Γυλιάμος (4365 ff.)

'and they found that the Great Lord [the Duke of Athens] had gone to the Kingdom of France, whither Prince William had sent him'

> οὕτως καθὼς τὸ εἴχασιν συμβουλευτῇ εἰς τὸ πρῶτον (6640)

'just as they had first decided'

In two passages one of the MSS of the *Chronicle* has εἶχα+aor.

infin., the other ἤμουν + aorist participle, a clear indication that
εἶχα + aor. infin. is functioning as a pluperfect substitute:

5770   εἶχεν ἐρωτήσεινε   P   ἦτον ἐρωτήσοντα   H
       εἶχεν ἀποθάνει   P   ἦτον ἀποθάνοντα   H

The next step, which was only possible once ἔχω + infin. had been
superseded by periphrases with θέλω in a future sense, was to
use ἔχω + aor. infin. of action completed in the past, i.e. to replace the ancient perfect. There are already examples of this in
the *Chronicle*, e.g.

ὁ κάποιος Φράγκος εὐγενής, ἄνθρωπος παιδεμένος,
ἀπὸ τὴν πόλιν ἔχει ἐλθεῖ ἀπὸ τὸν βασιλέαν   (4900–1)

'Some noble Frank, an educated man, had come from the city
from the emperor'

The old future periphrasis with ἔχω + infin. still occurs in the
Chronicle, but significantly almost entirely in subordinate clauses
introduced by νά, e.g.

καὶ θέλω νὰ σᾶς ἔχω εἰπεῖ περὶ τοῦ ρόϊ Κάρλου   (6773)

'and I wish to tell you about King Charles' (an interesting conflation of two future periphrases belonging to different stages of
the language). In Machairas *Chronicle of the sweet land of Cyprus*
εἶχα + aor. infin. is regularly used as a pluperfect, e.g. εἶχεν
πεθάνειν, εἶχεν πιάσειν, τὸν πύργον τὸν εἶχαν πάρειν οἱ Τοῦρκοι
'the fort which the Turks had taken'. These are the earliest
examples of a construction which did not become firmly established until the seventeenth century, and which in modern Greek
provides one of the two alternative perfect forms ἔχω γράψει
and ἔχω γραμμένο 'I have written'.[5]

The language of the vernacular texts shows some uncertainty
in regard to personal endings, forms which today either belong
to different dialects or are found coexisting only in certain aberrant dialects being used side by side. Thus in the third person
plural of present indicative and both subjunctives -ουν and -ουσι
are found, in the corresponding tenses of imperfect and aorist
indicative -αν and -ασι (and occasionally the purist form -ον),
together with -οσαν, whose origin has been discussed (p. 36).
As final -ν was labile, we often find forms in -ουνε, -ανε, resulting
from an effort to keep the personal ending distinctive. In the

medio-passive even greater disorder reigns: side by side with the purist -όμην, -εσο, -ετο, we find -ούμουν, -ούσουν, -όταν (the origin of the vowel -ου is uncertain); side by side with the purist -όμεθα, -εσθε, -οντο we find -όμεστα (by analogy with second person plural), -εστε (by phonetic development), -ουνταν (occasionally the hybrid form -ούντασιν if this is not a false vulgarism in Prodromos' poems). In the aorist passive -θηκα replaces -θην (the determining factor is probably the lability of final -ν), and forms with -κ- appear side by side with those without -κ- in the other persons; thus in the third person plural we have -θησαν, -θηκαν, and -θήκασι. In the verbs with final accentuation – the old contract verbs – confusion between original -άω verbs and original -έω verbs has led to the development of a common paradigm, particularly in the medio-passive, e.g. φοβοῦμαι, φοβᾶσαι, φοβᾶται: but forms in -ιέσαι, -ιέται are also found, e.g. πουλειέται, ἀγωνιέσαι. The imperfect of verbs with final accentuation is variously formed; in -οῦσα, -οῦσας, -οῦσε etc. on the analogy of the 3rd person plural -οῦσαν; in-αγα, -αγας, -αγε, etc. Modern dialects show a great variety of formations for this tense, and the Asia Minor dialects have developed a number of patterns unknown elsewhere in the Greek speaking world.

The existence in early vernacular literature of so many alternative verbal forms poses problems to which at present we can give no answer. The purist forms may be eliminated as due to scholarly and literary influence. But did -ουν and -ουσι, -ετον and -οταν really coexist in living speech? They were certainly living forms in different parts of the Greek speaking world.[6] This brings before us the problem of the origin of the common spoken language of the nineteenth and twentieth centuries. Does it go back to a common spoken language of at any rate the urban population in late Byzantine times, which is reflected, however imperfectly, in the language of the early vernacular poetry? Or do these poets write in an artificial amalgam of forms belonging to different dialects, which they have heard on the lips of uneducated speakers? In other words is their poetry a kind of incompetent attempt to imitate living speech by men whose only familiar mode of expression was the literary language. To answer a blunt yes or no to any of these questions would be to oversimplify the matter. But I am inclined – along with many others – to suppose that there was in late Byzantine times a common spoken language in the capital and in urban areas linked with it, a common tongue in which a great many alternative forms, belonging historically to different dialects, were unacceptable. Men from all over the Greek world mingled in Constantinople as they did nowhere else.

In the sphere of syntax the most important development of the period is that all prepositions are now constructed with the accusative case. Thus in the Prodromic poems we find in successive lines (3.38–39) ἀπὸ τῆς ἐκκλησίας 'from the church' and ἀπὸ τὸν ὄρθρον 'from dawn'; in the *Chronicle of the Morea* we find μὲ τὸν ρόϊ 'with the King', μετ᾽ αὐτήν 'with her' (both in the sense of 'with, in the company of'), ἀπὸ τὸ ἄλογον 'from the horse', in two successive lines (2496/7) μὲ τὴν βουλὴν ὅπου εἶχεν 'with the plan he had' and μετὰ χαρᾶς 'with joy', ἐκ τὸν φόβον 'out of fear', ἀπάνω τους 'above them'; in *Libistros and Rhodamne* we find ἀπὸ χώραν 'from land', μὲ τὸ λιτάριν 'with the pebble', ἐκ τὰ δάκρυα 'from tears', in two successive lines (947–8) μὲ τὸ βουκέντριν 'with the ox-goad', μετὰ γραμμάτων 'with a letter'; in the *History of Belisarius* we find δίχως ταραχήν 'without disturbance', μὲ τὰ χρυσᾶ κουδούνια 'with golden bells', ἐκ τὴν χαρὰν 'from joy', μετὰ τὸν Βελισάριον (= with B.); in the poems of Dellaportas we find μὲ λύπην 'with grief', ἀντὶς ἐμέ 'instead of me', ἐκ τὴν πικρὰν τὴν συμφοράν 'from grievous woe'. As a result the ancient distinctions between μετά + gen. 'with' and μετά + acc. 'after', διά + genitive 'by means of' and διά + acc. 'on account of', κατά + gen. 'against' and κατά + acc. 'along, in accordance with', παρά + gen. 'from' and παρά + accus. 'contrary to, along', etc. were effaced. This is no doubt the explanation of the growth of compound prepositions, which is particularly marked in the period under discussion. When με(τά) + acc. takes over the sense of 'with', the old meaning of μετά + acc. is expressed by ὕστερ᾽ ἀπό and the like. Similarly μέσα εἰς replaces the lost ἐντός + gen. Some of the inherited prepositions pass out of use in this period, except in clichés; such are ἀνά, ἐπί (replaced by ἐπάνω εἰς), κατά, περί, πρό, πρός, σύν, ὑπέρ, ὑπό.[7]

In the matter of vocabulary, one has a first impression that the period under discussion saw an immense enrichment both by derivation and by borrowing, as well as a number of semantic changes. This impression is probably to some extent misleading. For the first time since men stopped writing their private letters in Greek in Egypt, we have an extensive corpus of texts written in a language approaching the vernacular. Much of what was previously not recorded in writing comes to the surface. It is now clear that most of the features first met with in the early vernacular literature from the twelfth century on are in fact of much more ancient date, though in the absence of contemporary evidence any attempt to date any one with precision is impossible. However certain classes of loan-words can be dated, e.g. terms of feudal law borrowed from French, which are not likely to have entered Greek in any number before 1204.

The derivational suffixes listed in the previous chapter continued productive, and certain other suffixes became increasingly productive, e.g. -ίτσι(ον), -ούτσι(ον), -ούτσικος (these two of Italian origin). Compound words of all kinds are very frequent. Many of them are clearly nonce-formations, which bear witness to the 'open-ended' character of the vocabulary of medieval and modern Greek. An examination of 100 lines each of various near-vernacular texts of the period shows the following compounds which appear to be new – in the absence of lexica to these and other medieval Greek texts an impressionistic treatment is all that is possible.

(a) *Prodromic poems*

ταντανοτραγάτης
πρωτοβαβά
φιλεύσπλαγχνος
ψυχοκρατῶ
κοντασφίκτουρος
τριψιδογαροπίπερον
ἁγιόθρουμβον
πρασομάρουλον
χρυσολάχανον
φρυγιοκράμβιν
καρικοκουκουνάρια
στραγαλοσταφίδες
τσουκαλολάγηνα
χουρδούβελα
καθαροκόσκινον
κηροστούπιν
πηγαδόσχοινον
χαμομηλέλαιον
ἀγριοσταφίδα
λυσσομάμμουδον
τραυματάλειμμα
λυκοκαυκαλιάζω
σπαταλοκρομμύδη

(a) *Prodromic poems*

μονόκυθρον
παστομαγειρία
μεσονέφριν

(b) *Chronicle of the Morea*

σαγιτολάσι
φτωχολογία
ῥουχολογῶ
ἀρχοντολόγι

(c) *Libistros and Rhodamne*

παιδόπουλος
ἡλιογεννημένος
μυριοχάριτες
λαμπροχρωματισμένος
ποθοακαταδούλωτος
ἐρημοτοπία
ἀντιπεριπλέκομαι
ἐρωτικοκάρδιος
λογισμομαχῶ
ὁλοανασκέπαστος
ἐρημότοπος

(c) *Libistros and Rhodamne*

θαλασσοβράχι
δαιμονογυρεύω

(d) *Kallimachos and Chrysorrhoe*

δακτυλιδόπουλος
χρυσογνήματος
παμπλούμιστος
μισθαργός
σφυρηλάτημα
ἀκροπύργωμα
λιθομάργαρος
πυργόδωμα

(e) *Imperios and Margarona*

ἀργυροπεταλᾶτος
χρυσοτσάπωτος
κιτρινόχρους
ἀγγελοσουσσουμίαστος
λαμποαρματωμένος
συσσελοαρματωμένος

(f) *Trojan War*

(the alleged adaptation of Benoît
de Ste Maure's poem, of which
only a small part has been published)

ξενοχάραγος
περιμουσειωμένος

(f) *Trojan War*

μυρεψικός
βαλσαμόλαιον
λιθομάργαρος

(g) *Achilleid*

φεγγαρομεγαλόφθαλμος
κοκκινοπλουμόχειλος
μαργαροχιονόδοντος
γλυκόσταμα
κοκκινομάγουλος
κρυσταλλοκιονοτράχηλος
στρογγυλοεμορφοπήγουλος
ζαχαρογλυκερᾶτος
ποθοπερίβολος
μοσχόδενδρον
ροδόσταμα
καρδιοφλόγιστος

(h) *Leonardos Dellaportas*

δολοσυκοφαντία
κλωθογυρίζω
συχνοαναστέναμα
ζηλοφθονία
εὐτυχοτυχία
πικροδυστυχία
μυρωσκορπίζω
ἐπινόμι
καρδιογνώστης
λαμποευδοξότατος
μεγαλοευγενέστατος

Similar lists could be prepared from other near-vernacular
texts. As in classical and Hellenistic Greek, the great majority
of these compounds are determinative, and the order of the elements is that of classical Greek, i.e. the governing element pre-
cedes the governed, if it represents a noun or adjective, and follows it if it represents a verb. There are however many exceptions
to this rule. In particular compounds with a first verbal element
become common during the period under discussion, e.g. γλει-
φομελοῦσα, σβηνοκάνδηλας 'candle-snuffer', σπαταλοκρομμύδης
'onion-washer', σχιζοχάρτης 'paper-cutter', κοψόρρινος 'with
nose cut off'. Compound verbs with a nominal first element

representing the object of the verb or some adverbial qualifica-
tion become very common, e.g. ψυχοκρατῶ, λυκοκαυκαλιάζω,
ῥουχολογῶ, λογομαχῶ. They are not necessarily, as they are in
earlier periods, denominatives formed from a compound noun.
In the later middle ages direct borrowings from Latin virtually
cease. Latin was no longer the vernacular tongue of any region
within the empire or outside its frontiers, its role as an official
or administrative language was limited. The Latin acclamations
at the imperial court and the Latin subscriptions to documents
issued by the imperial Chancellery are by now mere fossilised
survivals, like the Norman-French phrases used by English
lawyers. On the other hand the growing influence of western
Europe, and the administration by western European powers of
large regions of Greek speech, lead to extensive borrowings from
Italian – mainly Venetian dialect – and French.[8] These Romance
loan-words are mainly cultural borrowings, i.e. they are names
for imported objects and concepts, and do not replace existing
Greek words. We have no direct evidence, but it is reasonable
to suppose that Italian loan-words were particularly common
in areas under Venetian or Genoese rule, such as Crete, Euboea
and many of the Cyclades, French loan-words in areas under
French rule, such as the Peloponnese, and above all Cyprus.
Terms of feudal law and land-tenure tend to be borrowed from
French, those referring to arts and crafts, and nautical terms,
are more usually of Italian origin. The great majority of these
loan-words are nouns, and they are generally adapted to some
Greek pattern – exceptions are mainly titles and other quasi-
proper nouns such as μισίρ, μισέρ (=monsieur). Verbs are not
easily borrowed into Greek, because of the necessity of providing two stems. The relatively few verbs borrowed from Romance –
or formed from Romance loan-words – are formed with the
productive suffixes -άρω, -ίζω, -εύω to which regular aorist
stems correspond. In spite of the first impression conveyed by
certain texts, the extent of borrowing from Romance languages
at this period was limited. These loan-words seldom became as
much an integral part of the language as did the Latin loan-words
of an earlier period. In particular they provided hardly any productive suffixes used for derivation from Greek stems: such
Romance suffixes as -άδος, -έλλα, -έλλο, -έττο, -έσσα, -ῖνος are
scarcely used except in Romance loan-words. A check of 100
lines each from a number of early vernacular texts revealed the
following French and Italian borrowings:

Chronicle of the Morea	*Kallimachos and Chrysorrhoe*
καβαλάρος, καβαλαρός	ἐξόμπλιον (Fr. exemple)
μισίρ	
ρόϊ	*Belthandros and Chrysantza*
λίζιος (liege)	φλισκίνα (piscina)
κουγκεστίζω (regularly formed	
verb from loan-word κουγ-	*Trojan War*
κέστα)	τσάμπρα (chambre)
Libistros and Rhodamne	*Achilleid*
	φισκίνα
τέντα	κουρτέσα
σουκανιά	φάλκων

Comparison with the similar lists of new compound words on pp. 87–8 underlines the fact that the great extension of the Greek vocabulary evident in this period was attained mainly by the use of Greek resources and not by lexical borrowing, in spite of the prestige which French and Italian enjoyed as languages of government. The main exception to this general formulation is in connection with maritime terms. These are very largely of Italian origin, and were often taken over from Greek into Turkish, Arabic, and to a lesser degree Russian. They formed a part of the lingua franca, an international mercantile and maritime vocabulary – it has not the structural features of a language – used throughout the eastern Mediterranean and the Black Sea until the nineteenth century.[9]

1. On the early vernacular literature cf. Knös (1962), where a full bibliography will be found.

2. Rohlfs (1950) 54, 57–8, 65.

3. Mirambel (1961).

4. Sandfeld (1930) 180–185; Havránek (1966); Reichenkron (1962).

5. cf. on this development Aerts (1965) 178–183.

6. Chatzidakis (1905) 37.

7. On the history of the prepositions in medieval Greek there is much material to be found in Jannaris (1897) 365–399. But a systematic study of the usage of the various texts is still a desideratum. On the dative case and its replacements cf. Trapp (1965).

8. The principal study of loan-words in medieval Greek is still Triantaphyllidis (1909).

9. cf. Kahane and Tietze (1958).

5

GREEK IN THE TURKISH PERIOD

The capture of Constantinople by the Turks in 1453 and the end of the Byzantine Empire did not change significantly the conditions in which the Greek language was used. Tendencies previously existing were only strengthened. 'Serious' literature continued to be written exclusively in the learned tongue, or as near an approximation to it as authors could attain. Literature in the spoken tongue, or in a language with many features of the spoken tongue, was almost confined to poetry. This poetry was not folk-poetry. It may have been orally composed in some cases, but in general it was not. Its authors, and also its readers or hearers, often belonged to the most prosperous and cultured elements of society. But it did not enjoy the prestige which a composition in the literary tongue would have enjoyed. And therefore men were careless of its linguistic form. And in any case there was no standard of correct usage other than that of the grammarians, which was wholly inappropriate to literature in the vernacular. Just as some of Petrarch's contemporaries – and sometimes Petrarch himself – esteemed his boring and derivative Latin epic *Africa* above the Italian poems of the *Canzoniere*, so Greek society – for all the pleasure which we know it took in vernacular poetry – felt that it did not merit the care in copying and transmission that were given to works in the learned tongue.

But here the resemblance between Greece and Italy ends. By Petrarch's time Italy already had a national language – *lingua toscana in bocca romana* – though it was not exactly the mother tongue of any community. Greece had to wait until the nineteenth century for a national language, and indeed in a sense it has not got one yet. The story of the struggle to forge a national language for the new nation state belongs to the following chapter. In the meantime let us consider briefly the situation in the period from the middle of the fifteenth century until the end of the eighteenth.

The considerable emigration of Greeks from Constantinople to regions still outside of Turkish control probably helped the spread of the spoken language of the capital to more distant regions, and thus furthered the development of a common spoken language. But at the same time since this language was not the vehicle of a literature which enjoyed esteem, and was not taught in schools, its spread was hindered, and the maintenance of dialect differences encouraged. The Turkish administration favoured decentralisation and isolation of provinces one from another. And the same is true of the existence of many regions under western rule, each of which looked to Italy or France for cultural patterns rather than to Constantinople. The city was no longer the centre of a Greek-speaking empire. Its intellectuals, who played an important role in the administration of the Ottoman empire, worked in a foreign linguistic environment, and used the learned tongue. The only intellectuals in the Turkish-ruled provinces were the clergy, who felt themselves to be the heirs of the Byzantine empire and used its classicising literary language for all but the most ephemeral communications. This kind of purism was all the easier in Greece, since the divergence between the learned and the spoken tongue was much less than in countries of Romance speech.

What we therefore find in the centuries of Turcocratia is a series of centres of vernacular literature, each showing greater or less dialect features in its linguistic form. They are all outside of the Ottoman empire, not because men no longer composed poetry under the Turks – the klephtic ballads are evidence of a flourishing oral poetry – but because on the whole the literate elements of Greek society under the Ottomans were not interested in this kind of literature. And of course there were far fewer men able to read and write under the Turks than, say, under the Venetians. They were also cut off from the direct influences of the Renaissance which were so strong in Venetian Crete or Lusignan Cyprus.[1]

Moving from East to West, we begin with Cyprus, where dialect features early manifest themselves in vernacular literature.

The *Chronicle* of George Boustronios continues that of Makhairas. A collection of love poems in the manner of Petrarch is almost a pure dialect text.[2] Cypriot Greek was too divergent from that spoken by the majority of Greeks to form a practical base for a common literary language, just as the language of the early Sicilian poets could not have provided the foundation for the Italian language. In any case Cyprus was conquered by the Turks in 1571, after a long war, and vernacular literature was driven underground, to survive only as folk-literature.

The next centre was the Dodecanese, and in particular Rhodes. From here we have several poems by Emmanuel Georgillas at the beginning of the sixteenth century, and a collection of love songs, less directly Italian in manner than the Cypriot poems.[3] With the conquest of the Dodecanese in 1522 this literature too ceases.

The third and most important centre was Crete, which remained under Venetian rule until 1669. Many refugees from Constantinople settled there shortly after the fall of the city. A moving lament for the capture of Constantinople, often thought to be composed in Crete, is more probably Dodecanesian. But by the beginning of the sixteenth century, vernacular literature was flourishing in Crete.[4] Manuel Sklavos' poem on the earthquake of 1508 was composed immediately after the event. George Choumnos' metrical paraphrase of Genesis – still largely unpublished – dates from a decade or two earlier. The autobiographical poems of Stephanos Sakhlikis belong to the early sixteenth century, the poems of Marinos Phalieros and Ioannes Pikatoros, are not easily datable but probably belong to the same period, as does the *Apokopos* of Bergades, a vision of Hell entirely independent of Dante. There is also much minor poetry of the sixteenth century. By the end of the century we find the beginnings of a school of drama under strong Italian influence. The principal names are those of Georgios Chortatzis and Vintsentzos Kornaros. To one or other of these are to be attributed in all probability the tragedies *Erophile, Rodolinos, Zeno*, and the *Sacrifice of Abraham*, and the comedies *Katzourbos, Stathes, Fortunatos* and *Gypares*. Kornaros is also author of a long romantic narrative poem *Erotokritos*, which represents the high point of Cretan literature.[5] *The Beautiful Shepherdess* ('Η ὡραία βοσκοπούλα), a pastoral poem owing much to Italian influence but full of local colour, is probably to be dated in the early sixteenth century. The earlier of these Cretan texts are written in the inherited amalgam of spoken Greek and flosculi from the learned tongue characteristic of the popular poetry of the late Byzantine period, with only occasional and unsystematic use of dialect features. For instance *The Beautiful Shepherdess* uses both the common demotic and the Cretan forms of the enclitic personal pronoun in successive lines – ἡ ὀμορφιά τζη, τὸ κορμί της, the Cretan form ἴντα and the common demotic form τί of the interrogative pronoun, etc. By the time of Chortatzis and Kornaros a process of purification has taken place, and few specifically non-Cretan forms are to be found, although in the matter of vocabulary borrowings are freely made from the learned language. This new literary language in embryo is based on the spoken Greek of east Crete, but also admits west Cretan forms, e.g. third person plural present indicative of verbs in -ουσι as against east Cretan -ουν(ε), and in the imperfect and aorist -ασι as against east Cretan -αν(ε); west Cretan temporal augment where east Cretan uses the syllabic augment, ἤφυγα for ἔφυγα; negatived future in δὲν θὰ plus subjunctive as against east Cretan δὰ μὴ plus subjunctive. It will be seen that the west Cretan forms most commonly admitted are precisely those which are also current in common demotic. The *Erotokritos* shows the purest east Cretan dialect, but even here west Cretan and common demotic forms are not infrequent.[6]

With the capture of Candia by the Turks in 1669 this flourishing Cretan literature, and the new literary language based upon the spoken tongue of Crete, come to an end. Cretan is not an archaic and peripheral dialect like Cypriot, and Crete might well have been the Toscana of modern Greece. But the disunity of the Greek-speaking world, and the lack of prestige of vernacular literature as compared with that in the learned tongue, as well as the general low cultural level of the Greek communities in the Ottoman empire, made the situation of Greece fundamentally different from that of Italy. The snuffing out of Cretan Greek literature in the second half of the seventeenth century only made impossible what had been in any case highly improbable.

A fourth centre of Greek literature was in the Ionian islands, held by Venice until the Napoleonic wars, and never subject to the Ottoman empire. In the sixteenth century we have poems by Koroneas of Zakynthos and Ioannes Trivolis of Corfu, a paraphrase of the *Iliad* in semi-vernacular Greek by Loukanios of Zakynthos, an adaptation of the *Theseid* of Boccaccio by an unknown poet, and a number of other works. After 1669 many Cretans fled to the Ionian islands bringing with them their songs and their literary tradition. But by this time the upper classes of the Ionian islands, so close to Italy and on the main trade routes of Venice, had become Italianised. Italian rather than Greek was the language of public intercourse in Corfu and the other towns. Hence there was not the urban public for vernacular literature that there had been in Crete. But Greek poetry, and the common language in which it was composed, survived among the country people and was by them communicated from time to time to the Italianate society of the towns. When, under the twin influences of the Romantic movement and the struggle for national liberation, the generation of Dionysios Solomos (1798–1857) sought to break away from the dead hand of the Byzantine learned language and to create a new national language for the renascent Greek people, based on the spoken tongue, they found in the Ionian islands of which Solomos and others were natives, a living tradition of literature in vernacular Greek, which, though it survived on the lips of humble peasants, went back through Venetian Crete and the vernacular literature of the late Byzantine world to the first creative break-through of the spoken tongue in the twelfth century.

In addition to works of literature we have one or two descriptions of the spoken language from this period. The earliest is the grammar by Nikolaos Sophianos of Corfu, written in the first half of the sixteenth century.[7] There are grammars by Girolamo Germano (1622)[8] and Simon Portius (1632).[9] These all include elements from the learned language, and Sophianos describes specific features of his native dialect. But they nevertheless provide – and this is particularly true of Sophianos – a coherent account of a common spoken language with variants. At the beginning of the eighteenth century Alessio de Somavera (Father Alexis de Sommevoir, a French Capuchin from Haute-Marne who spent many years in Constantinople, Smyrna and elsewhere in the Greek-speaking world) published the first lexicon of vernacular Greek.[10]

The main features of modern Greek had already taken shape before the fifteenth century. There are no phonological changes to record from the Turkish period, though no doubt in the process of dialect differentiation they did occur. One of the effects of the diglossy of the period was the existence of two phonological systems, one native to the spoken tongue, the other occurring in the numerous lexical borrowings from the learned language. The main point of difference is the treatment of $-\kappa\tau-$, $-\chi\theta-$ and $-\pi\tau-$, $-\phi\theta-$, preserved in learned loan-words, changed to $-\chi\tau-$ and $-\phi\tau-$ in the spoken tongue.

In the sphere of morphology we find, so far as our texts permit us to draw general conclusions, a general tightening up of the noun paradigm and elimination of anomalies and variant forms. But all texts, even the relatively homogeneous east Cretan of the Erotokritos, show many borrowings from the learned language or from earlier or geographically distinct forms of the spoken tongue, which bring their own morphology with them. One noteworthy regularisation is that of the stress accent in noun and adjective. The dialects still vary in their treatment of this. But the common demotic pattern whereby the accent shifts in the substantive according to ancient Greek rules, but remains immobile in the adjective, predominates in the period under review. Thus we have ἄνθρωπος, ἄνθρωπον, ἄνθρωποι (ἀνθρῶποι is 'vulgar') against ἀνθρώπου, ἀνθρώπους, ἀνθρώπων, but ὄμορφος, ὄμορφη, ὄμορφον, ὄμορφους, etc.

In the definite article the accusative plural feminine τές is more and more frequently replaced by τίς, the normal form in common demotic. But in dialects the older forms τές and even τάς still survive. The change from τές to τίς is probably due to the analogy of the other feminine forms ἡ, τή, τής, which proved stronger than that of feminine substantives in -ες.[11]

There are more changes to record in verb morphology. The future periphrasis in θὰ plus subjunctive, of which the earliest recorded example is probably in the Prologue of the *Chronicle of the Morea* (v. 825), replaces almost completely all other periphrases in the common spoken language, though other periphrases are found in dialects. In fact one can trace the spread of θὰ plus subjunctive at the expense of other patterns even into the dialects of Asia Minor and the curious dialect of Mariupol. In the period under review the Cretan drama and the *Erotokritos* both use θὰ plus subjunctive, though in Cretan dialects today, as almost certainly in the seventeenth century, other patterns are in use instead of or side by side with that in θὰ plus subjunctive.[12]

Two perfect periphrases become established, that in ἔχω plus the aorist infinitive (cf. p. 84), and that in ἔχω plus the perfect participle in -μένος, each having a nuance of its own. The latter is of course only formed from transitive verbs, and is in any case

4

much less frequent in demotic than the former. In the dialects the position is more complex. In some of the peripheral dialects ἔχω plus aorist infinitive is not used. In others a third form is found in ἔχω plus a verbal adjective in -τός. In the Pontic and Cappadocian dialects of Asia Minor neither is found, the perfect being expressed by the aorist indicative accompanied by the rigidified third person singular imperfect of the verb 'to be'; this is probably a relatively recent development due to Turkish influence.[13]

Side by side with the future in θά plus subjunctive we begin to find a potential mood formed by θά plus imperfect or aorist indicative. The new potential or conditional form in θά plus imperfect or aorist indicative replaces the medieval Greek form εἶχα plus aorist infinitive, which was left isolated once ἔχω plus aorist infinitive had lost its future sense and had become a perfect equivalent. An intermediate stage, or perhaps better a blind alley, is represented by νά plus past tense of the indicative, e.g. Prodromic poems (3.211) καὶ τότε νὰ 'δες, δέσποτα, πηδή-ματα νεωτέρου 'and then, lord, you will see the springing of a youth'. This construction was supported by the use of νά plus subjunctive as a future equivalent, itself probably arising out of the use of aorist subjunctive in future sense in Hellenistic Greek. The curious future form found in some dialects today, e.g. in Cretan, νά plus subjunctive plus θέλω (inflected) or rigidified θέλε, is probably due to conflation of this νά-future and the common demotic future formed with θά plus subjunctive. But there is still much that is uncertain in the development of future and conditional forms in modern Greek, owing to the ambiguous nature of the literary sources, the relative absence of dialect texts until the later nineteenth century, and the many gaps in our knowledge of modern Greek dialects today.

There are no changes in syntax to record in the Turkish period so far as common spoken Greek is concerned, other than those at a purely stylistic level, and those already discussed in connection with the formation of periphrastic tenses. In certain of the dialects, however, radical changes took place under the influence of the foreign linguistic environments in which they found themselves spoken. This is particularly true of many of the Asia Minor dialects, a great many of whose speakers were perforce bilingual. Though we have no dialect texts from the period, it is clearly during the centuries between the Turkish conquest and the first recording of dialect texts in the nineteenth century that such

changes took place as the adoption of Turkish word-order, with
the verb at the end of the sentence, the limitation of the use of
the definite article to the accusative, in which case Turkish too
distinguishes between definite and indefinite, the suppression of
grammatical gender and its attendant syntactic feature of agree-
ment, the development of a syntactical distinction between animate and inanimate substantives, etc.[14] The Greek enclaves in
Calabria and Apulia were similarly influenced by Italian. But
since the structural differences between Greek and Italian are
less striking than those between Greek and Turkish, the changes
are less radical. To Italian influence must be attributed such
features as the periphrastic passive formed with the verb 'to be'
and a passive participle, that formed with the verb *erkome*
(ἔρχομαι) and a passive participle on the model of Italian *venne
ucciso*, the absence of a distinctive future form, there being none
in the South Italian dialects of the surrounding areas, etc.[15]
Similarly the now almost extinct Greek of Cargèse, introduced
into Corsica by emigrants from Mani in the seventeenth century,
has been influenced in its syntactic structure by the Italian dialect
of Corsica and by French. It is too early to say whether similar
changes are taking place in the Greek of the Cypriot community
in London – and in any case it falls outside the period under discussion. But interesting observations have been made in this
connection regarding the speech of the Greek community of
Chicago.[16]

In vocabulary the principal source of new words continues to
be derivation and composition. Most of the suffixes productive
in the later middle ages continue to be productive in the Turkish
period. Some, like -άδα (abstracted from Italian dialect loan-
words), -ίτσι, -ίτσα, -ίτσης (probably not from Slavonic loan-
words, which never seem to have been numerous, but rather by
palatalisation of the consonant from -ίκι(ος)), became particularly
productive. Two suffixes abstracted from Turkish loan-words became productive, -τζής and -λῆς. Among new compound words
we find a great many compound verbs with a substantival or
adjectival first element, but to which no compound substantive
or adjective corresponds, e.g. γλυκοκοιτάζω, ψευτοζῶ. In
classical and Hellenistic, and generally in early Byzantine Greek,
compound verbs are either formed with an adverbial first element,
or as denominative verbs from a compound substantive or adjective. Another type of compound which first appears in late Hellenistic Greek and which becomes particularly frequent in the

period under review is the so called *dvandva* compound, e.g. γιδοπρόβατα 'goats and sheep', μερόνυχτο 'day and night'.

Loan-words from the Romance languages of the Mediterranean continue to enter Greek, particularly in regions under western political control. European cultural words are usually borrowed in their Italian form, occasionally in their French form. A new source of loan-words is Turkish. The Greek of mainland Greece and Asia Minor of the period becomes filled with Turkish words, in the first place social, political and religious terms, but also, and particularly in Asia Minor, where the Greek-speaking population was often bilingual, extending to all areas of the vocabulary. Turkish loan-words in common demotic are almost exclusively substantives; they are adapted to Greek morphology as neuters in -ι or in -ές if they are names of things, and as masculines in -ᾶς or -ῆς if they are names of persons. The Asia Minor dialects, being under longer and closer Turkish influence, have not only a great many more Turkish loan-words than common demotic but actually borrow Turkish verbs, which are adapted in various ways to the requirements of Greek morphology. The following list of Turkish loan-words, all of which are still in living use today, though the occasions for the use of many of them have become infrequent, give an idea of semantic spheres in which such loan-words were commonest.[17]

House, household goods etc.

κονάκι 'hostelry'
σεντούκι 'trunk'
σοφρᾶς 'table'
φυτύλι 'wick'
τουλούμι 'leather bottle'
τέντζερες 'cauldron'

Clothing and personal effects etc

φέσι 'fez'
γελέκι 'waistcoat'
γιακᾶς 'collar'
παπούτσια 'shoes'

Food and drink

πιλάφι 'pilaf'
γιαούρτι 'yoghourt'

Food and drink

γιαχνί 'dish of tomatoes and onions'
καπαμᾶς 'casserole of meat and tomatoes'
καφές 'coffee'
ναργιλές 'nargileh'
χαλβᾶς 'halva'

Man and family

μπόϊ 'statute'
νάζι 'archness'
κέφι 'humour'
λεβέντης 'handsome youth'
ἀφέντης 'effendi'

Military and administrative

τουφέκι 'rifle'

Military and administrative	Arts and crafts
μπαρούτη 'gun-powder'	γλέντι 'party, celebration'
γιαταγάνι 'yataghan'	τέλι 'wire'
παρᾶς 'coin'	ἀμανές 'oriental song'
χατζῆς 'hadji'	λαβοῦτο 'lute'

Significant absentees from this list are agricultural and pastoral terms, animal and plant names, general geographical and topographical terms, and abstract terms. Turkish influence was exerted through the towns, and not in the agricultural countryside, as was Slavonic influence, or in the mountain pastures, as was the influence of the Vlachs.

It is in texts of this period, though not in the poetic texts which approach most closely to the vernacular, that we first meet those linguistic calques, i.e. adaptation of Greek words, whether in their popular or their literary form, to cover the whole of the semantic field of a foreign word – usually French in this case – only part of which they previously covered, and formation of new Greek words by composition or derivation expressly as translations of foreign words. Examples of the former are ἔκφρασις 'expression', ἐξασκεῖ ἐπιρροήν 'il exerce une influence', of the latter ἐγκυκλοπάιδεια 'encyclopédie'. The second process has a unique aspect in Greek, inasmuch as modern Greek scientific terminology consists largely of compounds formed from Greek elements designed to correspond to French or English compounds, themselves formed from Greek elements. This means that a great many Greek compound words are first formed in a language other than Greek. There is a similar situation in regard to Chinese compounds first found in Japanese. The question of calques and of Greek words of foreign origin will be taken up in detail in the discussion of the vocabulary of present-day Greek.

1. On the Greek vernacular literature of the Turkish period cf. Knös (1963), where a full bibliography will be found; Dimaras (1967) and vols. 2 and 3 of Politis (1965–7) contain extensive excerpts from most of the texts mentioned and many others, with full references to manuscripts and editions.

2. Edited with French translation and full introduction by Siapkaras-Pitsillides (1952).

3. These are edited by Hesseling and Pernot (1913) and by Pernot (1931).

4. On this Cretan literature cf. Embiricos (1960), as well as the works by Knös (1963) and Dimaras (1967) cited above. There is a useful bibliography by M. Manoussakas (1953). In English the best introduction is Morgan (1960).

5. The best edition of the *Erotokritos* is still that of A. Xanthoudides (Heraklion 1915), with a long introduction and a study of the language. The text of Xanthoudides without his introduction and commentary has been reprinted in paper-back form (Athens 1962).

6. On the language of the *Erotokritos* cf. the chapter by G. N. Chatzidakes in Xanthoudides' edition. There are also many interesting observations in the rich but rather chaotic book of Pankalos (1955–60).

7. Ed. Legrand (1874).

8. Ed. Pernot (1907).

9. Ed. Meyer-Lübke (1889).

10. Alessio da Somavera (1709); cf. Legrand (1918) 74–77.

11. On the development of the definite article cf. Anagnostopoullos (1922), where a great deal of illustrative material is collected.

12. Pankalos (1955–60) I, 322–324.

13. Aerts (1965) 168–183.

14. Mirambel (1955), (1957–8), (1963), (1964).

15. Rohlfs (1950) 213–214, 220–221.

16. Seaman (1965).

17. The list is substantially taken from Costas (1936) 119–120.

6

THE DEVELOPMENT OF
THE NATIONAL LANGUAGE[1]

In the late middle ages and the early centuries of the Turkish period the common spoken language of the Byzantine empire lived on, but tended more and more to become regionally differentiated. It was impoverished in abstract terms and ill-adapted to serve as a vehicle of higher culture. The Greek upper classes of Constantinople and of other cities in the Ottoman empire, and the Orthodox church, used for all official and literary purposes the traditional learned language, which was essentially late Atticising Koine. New literary languages, based upon the dialects of particular regions but strongly influenced by the common spoken language began to be formed in parts of the Greek world where the conditions favoured an active cultural life. The only one of these to attain any degree of maturity was that of the Cretan literature of the sixteenth and seventeenth centuries. But even in Crete the favourable conditions did not last long enough for a national language, parallel to those of western Europe, to arise.

As the national consciousness of the Greeks deepened in the closing decades of the eighteenth centuries, and as the question of liberation from the Turkish yoke and the establishment of a modern nation state came on the order of the day, the need for a genuine national language came to be felt and discussed. Both in Greece itself, and even more in the large and prosperous Greek colonies in Russia and western Europe, more and more

books were being published, works on science and technology
were being translated or composed in Greek. These were written
in various mixtures of spoken Greek and the literary language,
without any marked dialect features, but with little unity of form.

It was against this background that the Language Question,
which has been in the forefront of Greek cultural and political
controversy ever since, was first posed.[2] A number of answers
were given at the end of the eighteenth century and the beginning
of the nineteenth. The conservatives, who were against the struggle for liberation and preached obedience to the Sultan, the
sovereign set over the Greek people by God, were naturally
linguistic conservatives also. For them the only national language
was the traditional learned language, as used by the Phanariot
nobility and the Orthodox hierarchy. Their spokesman, P.
Kodrikás, had few followers, and the tendency which he represented seemed doomed to failure. In fact, by the irony of history, many of his aims were realised by his bitterest opponents,
as we shall see.

Among those who equated nation and people, and who therefore favoured a national language based on the speech of the
people, there were various tendencies. Some, who were influenced
by western rationalism and classicism, saw in the speech of the
Greeks of their own time a form of ancient Greek corrupted by
centuries of slavery. For them the only possible course was to
write off the Middle Ages and to go back to ancient Greek as the
true national language. This somewhat utopian programme they
believed could be realised once national independence had been
attained. Then the Greek people, who had been the leaders and
teachers of the world, would regain its rightful position and
speak with its true voice. Needless to say, nothing which could
be called literature resulted from this movement. Its leading
figures were Eugenios Voulgaris (1716–1806), Stephanis Kom-
metas (†1814), Dimitrios Darvaris (1757–1823), Neophytos
Doukas (*c.* 1760–1845), Konstantinos Oikonomos (1780–1857).

Another group, at whose head stood the patriot and scholar
Adamantios Korais (1743–1833), took the spoken language of
their own time as their starting point, but wished to purify it.
This purification was not to be limited to the rejection of Turkish
loan-words and of the more aberrant dialect features, but was to
extend to phonology, morphology and syntax. Only a language
capable of expressing all the nuances of meaning, and equally
understood by all, was a suitable instrument for the intellectual

emancipation of the people. This 'purified' spoken Greek was to
be the vehicle of education in the new Greece, freed from the
Turkish yoke. Archaism, kicked out by the door, was coming
in by the window. Korais' purified spoken Greek was sometimes
remarkably like the traditional language of his opponent Kodrikás, though there were a number of shibboleths by which they
could be distinguished. To take an example, 'fish' in common
spoken Greek is ψάρι; Korais would introduce the 'pure' (i.e.
archaistic) form ὀψάριον, while the extreme archaists and Kodrikás would alike favour ἰχθύς, the classical word. The only important literary monument of Korais' school was the collection
of his own letters, published after his death. But the influence of
his ideas, often seized upon in a partisan fashion which he would
have himself disowned, was great in the half-century after his
death.

A third group, inspired by belief in democracy and conscious
that it was upon the basis of the 'unpurified' vernacular speech
that most western European national languages had been built,
wished to turn their backs on the traditional learned language
and to make the tongue of the common people the national
language, whose native resources would be developed to provide
the new terms necessary. This was what the poets of the Ionian
islands were already doing, and steps in this direction had already
been taken by writers like Mysiodax (1730–1800), Katartzis
(1720–1807) and others. One of the problems was the lack of
uniformity of the spoken tongue. Ioannes Vilaras of Jannina
(1771–1823) published his Romaic Grammar in 1814, seeking to
codify rigorously the orthography, morphology and syntax of
the vernacular in order to fit it to play its new role as a national
language and the vehicle of national education. In spite of his
aims, his work is not free from dialect features.

This was the situation on the eve of the Uprising of 1821, as a
result of which a Greek state was created. During the years of
the war of liberation there were considerable movements of
population, as revolutionary fighters from various parts of Greece
and from Greek communities abroad came together, in particular
in the Peloponnese. It was in the Peloponnese, at Nauplion, that
a provisional administration was set up in 1828, around which
there gathered emigrants from Constantinople as well as Greeks
from every region of Greece. There grew up there in those years
a new common language, based on the dialects of the Peloponnese, but with a good many Ionian features. Peloponnesian

Greek was well fitted to be the basis of a national language. Without either the radical phonetic changes of northern Greek or the archaic features of Cretan or Cypriot, it was easily understood by all Greeks, and was sufficiently close to the language of late Byzantine and post-Byzantine vernacular literature to be acceptable to all as a common tongue. And in addition the distinguished part played by the Peloponnesians in the war of liberation gave it a new prestige in the eyes of their contemporaries. Thus when in 1833 Athens became the capital of the new state, it was the Peloponnesian koine that became the language of ordinary intercourse among the new citizens who flocked thither from every part of the Greek world. The native population of Athens, which in any case scarcely reached 10,000, was swamped by the newcomers, and the dialect of Athens, which belonged to a rather archaic group spoken in Attica, the Megarid, Aegina and parts of Euboea, was soon replaced by the common spoken tongue.

It might have been expected that this common spoken tongue, with a Peloponnesian basis, would be gradually freed from the traces of the dialect of the Ionian islands which it still retained, and would become the national language, used for official purposes, in education, and in literature of all kinds. But things turned out otherwise. The years after the establishment of the state of Greece were a period of political reaction, during which the ruling class rejected the rationalist and democratic spirit which had animated the generation of the liberation. This ruling class consisted to an ever-growing degree of wealthy Phanariots from Constantinople and their hangers-on, men wedded to the traditional learned tongue, and fearful of the political implications of its rejection in favour of the speech of the mass of the people. Under their influence archaism became the order of the day. Korais' conception of the 'purification' of the language of the people was carried to absurd extremes, and put into effect in a spirit very different from that of Korais. Poetry continued to be written mainly in the demotic – and in any case the Ionian islands, where Solomos still lived and wrote, did not form part of the Kingdom of Greece and were relatively immune to the baneful influence which spread from Athens. But even in this context it is significant that Valaoritis (1824–1879), a native of Levkas and a relation of Solomos, whose literary heir and successor he became, saw fit to accompany his poems in demotic with a commentary in the archaising katharevousa. For it is in this period that the diglossy which, as we have seen, existed in the Greek-speaking world from Hellenistic times, took the form in which we are familiar with it today, a polarisation into demotic and katharevousa. This katharevousa is not the traditional Atticising Koine of Byzantine culture, which was at least the language of organisations and institutions which had remained in existence through centuries and millennia, though few children ever learned it at their mother's knee – we may perhaps make an exception for the children of Anna Comnena, the imperial historian of the twelfth century, who was so proud of her archaising and erudite language. The katharevousa was created in the second quarter of the nineteenth century by progressive 'purification' of the new demotic, and introduction of more and more elements from the learned tongue. It is always macaronic in character, mingling together incongruously old and new, and studded with false archaisms, hypercorrect forms, and mere blunders. This was the language used for administration and education, in journalism and public life, and in almost all prose writing, literary or scientific, until the end of the nineteenth century. It had to be learned as a foreign language, it was imprecise, vacuous and inordinately fond of calques, and its existence and the prestige which it enjoyed did much to hold back the intellectual and artistic development of the people. It was never uniform. Some writers used the ancient Greek future forms, not always correctly, others the periphrastic future in θὰ of demotic, others θέλω plus infinitive; the dative case, obsolete ancient Greek prepositions, the negative particle οὐ etc. were used to a varying degree by different writers and by the same writer on different occasions. Writers and speakers watched one another narrowly and critically, ready to seize upon the least concession to 'the vulgar tongue'. There were extreme archaisers like the lexicographer S. Vyzantios and the novelist, dramatist and grammarian Panayotis Soutsos, who wanted to restore ancient Attic – the former thought it would take 100 to 150 years, the latter believed thirty years enough![3] And there were moderates like Asopios, Trikoupes and Mavrophrydes who saw some virtue in the popular tongue. But all alike were engaged in a contest of purity – like so many different brands of detergent – in which one had to go further than one's rivals. So for a phrase like 'if I cannot', we find a series of more and more 'pure' renderings, which depart more and more from the linguistic feeling of the ordinary Greek: ἄν δὲν μπορῶ (normal spoken Greek) ἄν δὲν ἠμπορῶ (old-fashioned spoken Greek, or dialect) ἂν δὲν δύναμαι, ἐὰν δὲν δύναμαι, ἐὰν μὴ δύναμαι, ἐὰν μὴ δύνωμαι. Similarly 'when he arrived' passes through the successive stages ὅταν ἔφτασε, ὅταν ἔφθασε, ὅταν ἀφίχθη, ὅτε ἀφίχθη, ὅτε ἀφίκετο. Paradigmatic patterns are confused. Thus the verb 'bring' has a present theme φέρν- and an aorist theme φερ-: φέρνεις ~ ἔφερες. The purist, worried by the fact that φερ- is a present theme in ancient Greek, uses ἔφερες as an imperfect instead of an aorist; so he has to resuscitate the long-obsolete aorist ἤνεγκας (or -ες) to complete the paradigm. From there it is but a step to such choice morsels of archaism as ἐνεχθείς. Not only were foreign loan-words replaced by words of Greek derivation, but perfectly good Greek words too were replaced by what were thought to be their classical equivalents: χαμογελῶ 'smile' became μειδιῶ, χιονίστρα 'chilblain' became χείμετλον, ἐμεῖς and ἐσεῖς became ἡμεῖς and ὑμεῖς, which are homophonous! These archaic words brought their archaic morphological system with them, instead of being adapted to the morphology of modern Greek.

The learned language had not in the past been generally used to describe the details of everyday life. The principles of ancient rhetoric, by which the Byzantines were guided, enjoined the avoidance of the trivial, the humble and the banal, and above all of the particular; one did not call a spade a spade, any more than did Tacitus in Latin – when he had to refer to it, he called it *per quae terra egeritur*. The katharevousa, if it was to serve as a national language for all purposes, had to have a word for everything. The existing terms of demotic were often morphologically or otherwise incompatible with the katharevousa, and there were no traditional learned terms. So fantastic pseudo-archaic words had to be invented. A nutcracker (τσακιστήρι) became καρυοθραύστης, καρυοκλάστης or καρυοκατάκτης, a corkscrew (τιρ-μπουσόνι) became ἐκπώμαστρον, the back of a chair (ράχη) became ἐρεισίνωτον, a blind alley (τυφλοσόκακο) became ἀδιέξοδον, a safe (κάσσα) became χρηματοκιβώτιον, a potato (πατάτα) became γεώμηλον, itself a calque of French *pomme de terre*, a chamber-pot (καθίκι) became οὐροδοχεῖον, and so on.

Manipulation of katharevousa in its extreme form demanded a good knowledge of ancient Greek at the levels of morphology, syntax and vocabulary, as well as acquaintance with a multitude of arbitrary neologisms. It was in vain that generations of schoolmasters tried to teach their pupils to speak and write it.

Their lessons were rendered all the less effective by the fact that the schoolmaster himself, when he was not in the classroom, spoke the same demotic as everyone else. The result of all this was the creation of a new diglossy, related to that of the Byzantine epoch, but essentially different, inasmuch as the new learned language was supposed to be used by the whole community. In fact, if we take into account the fact that the majority of Greeks in the nineteenth century spoke their local dialect rather than common demotic in most situations, the situation can better be described as triglossy. It was a situation which hindered self-expression and communication, prevented the study and development of the resources of the mother-tongue, and favoured the muddled, the ambiguous and the half-understood.

By the end of the nineteenth century the influence of the Phanariots had declined, a new native bourgeoisie was growing up, universal education was producing a literate population which had nothing to read, and a generation of scholars and critics trained in France and Germany was interesting itself in the history of the Greek language – the katharevousa had no history. At the same time interest in the folklore of Greece was leading to a corresponding interest in the spoken language, dialect texts, folk-songs and the like. It was under the influence of these and other factors that Jean Psichari (1854–1929) developed his linguistic ideas. He wished to end the use of katharevousa and make a codified and systematised demotic the only national language. Demotic would have to borrow from katharevousa vocabulary elements necessary for philosophical, literary and scientific discourse, but these would without exception be adapted to demotic phonological and morphological patterns. At the same time the orthography, while remaining basically historical rather than phonetic, would be tidied up and regularised. His novel Τὸ ταξίδι μου, published in 1888, was the first serious literary prose in demotic, and it created a furore. In his eagerness to produce a regularised and codified demotic, Psichari often neglected the existence of doublets in the Greek vocabulary, e.g. δουλεία 'slavery' and δουλειά 'work, affair', θεωρία 'theory' and θωριά 'face', στοιχεῖο 'element' and στοιχειό 'monster', ἐργαλεῖο 'tool' and ἀργαλειό 'loom', πραγματεία 'scientific study' and πραμάτεια 'commodity', χωρίο 'passage in a book' and χωριό 'village'. And just as the purists invented false archaisms, so he occasionally invented false demoticisms, e.g. περκεφαλιά for περικεφαλαία 'helmet'. And by extending certain derivational

suffixes of demotic to new semantic fields he sometimes produced
a ridiculous effect: e.g. there are many abstract nouns in -άδα, a
suffix of Venetian origin, e.g. νοστιμάδα 'savour, pleasantness'.
When its use was extended to replace the learned -ότης, -ισμός
in such words as κλασικάδα, this offended against the linguistic
feeling of Psichari's contemporaries. In fact, as we shall see,
current demotic usage does not automatically adapt its numerous
borrowings from katharevousa to demotic phonology and morphology, and readily tolerates coexistence of two or even more
rival patterns.

Psichari, who was a philologist of distinction, based his preference for the spoken tongue on historical and linguistic considerations.[4] For most of his opponents, as well as for some of
his followers, less rational and more emotional motives determined their attitude. Many felt that the only bond linking the
Greeks of their own time to those of the Byzantine empire and
of classical antiquity was their language, and that if that was
given up, the national consciousness would wither away, and
Greece would be absorbed by her non-Hellenic neighbours. The
theory of the German scholar Fallmerayer, that the original
Greek population had been ousted by Slavonic immigrants in
the early middle ages, and that consequently the present-day
Greeks were only the cultural successors, and not the biological
descendants, of the ancient Greeks, though hotly contested by
most Greek scholars, frightened many people. Thus the Language
Question once more took on a political aspect, which it has retained ever since. Those who wished to replace the katharevousa
for literary, scientific and official use were accused by their
opponents of being traitors to their people and their church,
Freemasons and tools of the Panslavists. In more recent times
the charge against them has been of sympathy with Communism,
usually with the strong anti-Slavonic overtones which such a
charge has in Greece. In general the attitude of Greek govern-
ments to the Language Question has corresponded to their
position on the political spectrum – though there have been
exceptions to this rule. And it has always been possible to impugn
a man's political views and his national loyalty by pointing to
his use of language; at times this has degenerated into an un-
principled witch-hunt.

Popular interest in the Language Question has always been
high, though often not particularly well-informed. Pallis' demotic translations of the *Iliad* (1892–1904) and above all of the

New Testament (1902) provoked riots in Athens. And Greek readers sometimes give the impression of being more interested in the linguistic form than in the content of a book.

In spite of some hesitations by Psichari's contemporaries, demotic soon became the language of all literary prose. Style and linguistic form became distinct, and the new demotic prose soon developed great stylistic flexibility in the hands of novelists and short-story writers.[5] Journalism, scientific writing, and official writing – laws, proclamations, instructions on filling up forms, and so on – remained the province of katharevousa. And katharevousa continued to be both the language taught in schools and the language of instruction. But it was a changing katharevousa. More and more such extravagant archaisms as the optative, the ancient Greek future, imperatives in -θι; the so-called Attic declension, tended to be quietly given up; the dative became rare; and a great many demotic words were admitted, although dressed in katharevousa forms.

In 1917 demotic became both the subject of instruction and the medium of instruction in the lower forms of schools, and a whole series of demotic text-books had to be written. In 1921–23 a right-wing government restored katharevousa throughout the schools for two years. From 1923 till 1967 with a brief interval under the right-wing government of Tsaldaris in 1935–36 demotic continued to be the language of the lower forms of schools, with much hesitation in policy and variation of detail, and also with certain changes in the officially recognised linguistic form. In 1967 the military junta once again banned demotic completely from the schools. Now textbooks in katharevousa have to be written. And the Greek child on going to school is told that the way he and his family and every one he has ever known speak is wrong and must be 'corrected' by a continuous and unremitting effort – an effort which, he will be quick to observe, the schoolmaster does not make once he is out of the classroom. It is beyond the scope of this book to discuss the psychological results of such a system of education.[6] On the linguistic level it certainly contributes to imprecision, ambiguity, and loading of emotional significance on to the linguistic form, a significance which may be a much more important part of the message than its overt content of information.

While all literary writing for more than half a century has been in demotic, which has developed its resources enormously during this period, and while a somewhat less rigorous katharevousa continues to be the vehicle of all official pronouncements and transactions, and of most scientific and technical writing, there has grown up a kind of compromise linguistic form, often described as ἡ μικτή (or μιχτή) γλῶσσα, in the domain between the literary and the technical-official. It is particularly in the newspapers and weekly and monthly reviews that this μικτή, the outlines of which are blurred, finds its use. Indeed a Greek newspaper – before April 1967 – was linguistically a most interesting document. Official proclamations, public announcements, texts of laws etc. were in katharevousa. Editorial matter, literary criticism and the like were in literary demotic. The news pages were in various varieties of the mixed language, the more technical sections, e.g. financial news, inclining towards katharevousa, the sports pages affecting a more demotic tone.

While the basic distinction remains that between the common spoken language and an artificial, archaising language reserved for certain kinds of writing and of formal utterance, the simple, bipolar analysis of the Greek linguistic situation has been felt by many to be inadequate. A generation ago Professor André Mirambel, in an epoch-making article,[7] suggested that neither katharevousa nor demotic had any real internal unity. For him Greek is 'un ensemble d'usages linguistiques qui tantôt s'opposent, tantôt se combinent'. In spite of its millenary external cohesion, Greek has little inner cohesion. Mirambel identifies five 'états de langue' in use in contemporary Greece:

(1) The katharevousa, the official language of state, army and administration. It avoids all that is not 'pure Greek' and consecrated by ancient written texts. But it has changed greatly over the last half-century. It is rich in adjectives and abstract nouns, addicted to formulae, practises an elaborate sentence-structure with several degrees of subordination, and readily forms calques of foreign terms. It enjoys still the reputation of corresponding to a higher degree of culture than other linguistic forms. No one speaks it regularly or consistently, and there are many situations in which its use is impossible, e.g. the most uncompromising purist would not make love in katharevousa. Yet it appears as the consecration of privilege and the guarantee of established order.

(2) The μικτή is structurally similar to the katharevousa, but avoids some of its extreme archaisms. It accepts indispensable terms from the spoken language without modification of their

form, and thus juxtaposes heterogeneous forms. It is used both
in writing and in speech, in the latter case often by those who try
to speak katharevousa. It is the language of scientific and technical writing, of much journalism, and of political speeches.[8]

(3) The καθομιλουμένη, on the other hand, is demotic supplemented heavily by elements from the learned tradition. It
admits most of the spoken forms and words, rejecting only some
neologisms. It, too, has heterogeneous forms side by side. Thus
it uses the spoken forms ἡ βρύση, τῆς βρύσης 'spring', ἡ νεότητα,
τῆς νεότητας 'youth', but in technical or abstract terms it preserves the purist morphology, thus ἡ ἀναγέννησις, τῆς ἀναγεν-
νήσεως 'renaissance', ἡ ἐθνικότης, τῆς ἐθνικότητος 'nationality'.
It says ἑστία rather than τζάκι for 'hearth, household', because
the latter word has a 'peasant' tone. It says ἅλας for 'salt' in
the chemical sense, but ἅλατι in the culinary. In general words
and formulae from the learned language are freely adopted without morphological change. It is the language of the urban middle
classes and of Athenian society, with a wide range of spoken
uses, and growing use in journalism. It is the result of a conflict
between living and learned elements in subjects of a certain level
of culture, who wish to express themselves effortlessly, without
worrying about the uniformity of their linguistic usage.

(4) Δημοτική is the result of natural development of Greek
over the centuries, the language whose development has been the
main subject of this book. Its main characteristics are unifica-
tion of nominal flexion, abundance of compounds, which are
freely formed, a variety of new nominal and adjectival suffixes,
but only a few inherited verbal suffixes (mainly because of the
necessity of providing two themes for a Greek verb), many
loan-words, often treated as indeclinables, an invariable relative pronoun πού, many new compound subordinating conjunc-
tions, and a balance between synthetic and analytic structure.
This is the language of the mass of the people, and of all who
seek to speak naturally. It is also the language of almost all
creative writing, and is finding increasing use in abstract and technical writing; though in this latter use it tends to acquire the
slightly macaronic character of the καθομιλουμένη.

(5) Μαλλιαρή. This is a perjorative term used by purists to
describe a systematisation of δημοτική by grammarians, who
endeavour to choose between the many alternative forms available in demotic. It attempts to give added precision and clarity
to the often somewhat vague demotic, and often advocates a

reformed orthography, on phonetic rather than historic principles. This is no one's mother tongue, and grammars of it are
normative rather than descriptive.

Mirambel's analysis, made thirty years ago, is largely valid
today.[9] His fifth category is not really a state of the language
parallel to the others. And of the others, (1) and (2) are varieties
of katharevousa, (3) and (4) varieties of demotic. One may hesitate whether to class a sample text in (1) or (2), or in (3) or (4).
But one cannot read two lines without seeing whether it is a
variety of demotic or of katharevousa.

The changes which are taking place before our eyes are the
most difficult to detect. The following notes on the tendencies
in Greek in the last thirty years make no claim to be exhaustive.
The role of Mirambel's katharevousa is more and more confined
to official pronouncements, laws, railway timetables and the
like. Its functions in other situations are more and more taken
over by Mirambel's μικτή. In this slow change the new art or
science of publicity was a determining factor. It is very difficult
to engage the attention and interest of reader or hearer in katharevousa. The military regime which seized power in April 1967 is
committed to restoring katharevousa to its pristine glory, and
has made its use and study obligatory throughout schools. It
is too early to say whether their efforts will have any lasting result.
Curiously enough, another stronghold of more or less pure
katharevousa is technical literature, though here too the urgent
need of efficient communication forces the writers – or more
usually translators – of manuals to make a few concessions to
demotic. The hopes which used to be expressed in certain circles
that a kind of compromise between demotic and katharevousa
would become the true national language, used by all classes for
all purposes, are far from realisation.

New ideas are expressed either by calque or by loan-word.
Generally speaking, katharevousa uses calques, demotic uses
loan-words, but there are many complexities in practice. Examples of calques in katharevousa are: πόλεμος ἀστραπῆς 'blitz-
krieg', ἀπομαγνητίζω 'to degauss', παρεμβατισμός 'interven-
tionism', στρουθοκαμηλισμός 'ostrich policy', ἀεριωθούμενον
ἀεροπλάνον 'jet aircraft', διαστημόπλοιον 'space-ship'. These
calques are often taken over by demotic with a greater or less
degree of adaptation to demotic patterns. Loan-words in demotic
are either treated as indeclinable substantives, or are adapted

to Greek morphology. Examples of the former are ἀμπραιάζ, ἀμορτισέρ, μαρσεπιέ, μπάρ, μίς 'beauty-queen'. Examples of the latter are στοπάρω, στοπάρισμα, φρενάρω, φρενάρισμα, μιζεμπλιζάρω, μιζεμπλιζάρισμα 'hair-set'. It will be noted how frequent the verbal suffix -άρω and its derivative -άρισμα are in these recent adapted loan-words. There is a tendency for loan-words to pass from the first to the second category when they are in frequent use. Thus the written form, both in literature and journalism and on garage signs, is τό γκαράζ, but one hears τό γκαράζι. In technical manuals one often finds attempts at providing katharevousa equivalents for loan-words, but these words rarely enter into general use. Thus to demotic ἀσανσέρ 'lift' there correspond katharevousa ἀνυφωστής, ἀνελκυστής, but they are scarcely used. A concrete-mixer is ἡ μπετονιέρα – a loan-word adapted to Greek morphology; in technical manuals, but hardly anywhere else, one may find ὁ μαλακτήρ. The successful neologisms are those of demotic, or the katharevousa terms which have been taken over by demotic. The factors which determine their success or failure are often extra-linguistic. Thus though ὑπαρξισμός has replaced ἐξιστενσιαλισμός, often heard after the war, the pre-First World War term κοινωνισμός has been ousted by σοσιαλισμός. A rich source of neologisms is provided by the technical terms of international currency formed from Greek roots, which are readily adopted by Greek. An obvious example is κοσμοναύτης. But in order to be acceptable in Greek, these words have to be formed in accordance with Greek rules of derivation and composition. The international term is 'telegram', but Greek says τηλεγράφημα, the regular derivative from τηλεγραφῶ.

Words formed from Greek roots and adaptable to Greek morphological categories have a built-in linguistic advantage over phonologically awkward and indeclinable loan-words. It is this, rather than any purist preoccupations, which have led ποδόσφαιρο 'football' to outstrip φουτμπώλ in recent years. One may expect that in course of time a great many of the unmodified loan-words brought into Greek by the technological explosion of our age will be either adapted to fit a Greek morphological pattern or replaced by a calque, perhaps first formed in katharevousa.[10]

Though neither katharevousa nor demotic is fixed and unchangeable in form, each preserves its own identity – demotic all the more so since its standardisation by Triantaphyllides in 1940 and the subsequent use of this standardised demotic in the lower forms of schools until 1967. The various 'mixed' forms of speech turn out on inspection to be clearly demotic or katharevousa, with certain quite limited features of the other. Thus any katharevousa word may be borrowed by demotic, usually without morphological modification, but borrowings in the other directions are rare. The conversation of an educated person may contain not only katharevousa vocabulary, but a certain amount of katharevousa morphology and phonology, as he recollects and reproduces what he has read; but there is nothing systematic about this. Journalistic katharevousa often uses certain demotic forms from contract verbs, e.g. -ιέται for -εῖται, -οῦσα for -ουν or -ων. And so on. The tables below contain diagnostic features of katharevousa (K) and demotic (D). These are positive diagnostic features, whose presence is normally sufficient to identify the language of a sample text. They should enable any text in contemporary Greek to be identified as katharevousa or demotic, even if it contains some admixture of the other.

DIAGNOSTIC FEATURES OF K AND D

K	*D*
(A) *Phonology and orthography*	
Presence of final -ν in acc. sing., neuters in -ον, 1st person pl. in -ομεν etc.	Absence of final -ν
κτ, πτ, χθ, φθ	χτ, φτ
Shifting accent in adjectives e.g. νεωτέρα	Fixed accent in adjectives e.g. νεώτερη
(B) *Morphology*	
εἰς τόν etc. ἀπό τόν etc.	στόν etc. ἀπ' τόν etc. (not always indicated in writing)
Enclitic gen. pl. των	τους
	Verbal noun in -σιμο, -σίματος

K	D

(B) *Morphology*

-όμεθα	-όμαστε
-θην	-θηκα
-θης etc.	-θηκες
Unstressed augment	

-όμην	-όμεθα	-όμουν	-όμαστε
-εσο	-εσθε	-όσουν	-όσαστε
-ετο	-οντο	-όταν	-όνταν
in imperfect passive			

Imperfect of contract verbs

-ων	-ῶμεν		
-ας	-ᾶτε		
-α	-ων	-οῦσα	-ούσαμε
-ουν	-οῦμεν	-οῦσες	-ούσατε
-εις	-εῖτε	-οῦσε	-οῦσαν
-ει	-ουν		

Declined participles · Gerund in -οντας

(C) *Derivation*

K	D
-τήριος	-ένιος
-τέος	-ούλης
	-ούτσικος
	-άκι
	-άδα
-ως	-α (Adverbs)
-δην	
-άδην	
-δόν	
-αδόν	

(D) *Vocabulary*

K	D
Compounds in εὐ-, δυσ-, τρισ-, ἰσο-, ἡμι-, παν-, φιλο- etc.	Dvandva compounds, other than a few found in Byzantine Greek. In particular, verbal dvandvas are characteristic of demotic, e.g. ἀνοιγοκλείνω, τρωγοπίνω

K	D
εἶς	ἕνας
μέγας	μεγάλος
ἰχθύς	ψάρι
πτηνόν	πουλί 'bird'
κύων	σκύλος, σκυλί 'dog'
ὀστοῦν	κόκκαλο 'bone'
ὀφθαλμός	μάτι 'eye'
ῥίς	μύτη 'nose'
ἧπαρ	συκώτι 'liver'
ἵσταμαι	στέκομαι 'stand'
ὕδωρ	νερό 'water'
πῦρ	φωτιά 'fire'
ἐρυθρός	κόκκινος 'red'
θερμός	ζεστός 'hot'
ὄφις	φίδι 'snake'
ἄνθος	λουλούδι 'flower'
παγνύω	παγώνω 'freeze'
κόπτω	κόβω 'cut'
πλησίον	κοντά 'near'
ὠθῶ	σπρώχνω 'push'
ῥίπτω	ῥίχνω 'throw'
ὀσφραίνομαι	μυρίζομαι 'smell'
ἔτος, ἐνιαυτός	χρόνος 'year'
διότι	γιατί 'because'

1. On the whole of this chapter cf. Caratzas (1958).

2. Megas (1925), Kordatos (1943).

3. Triantaphyllides (1938) 97.

4. Mirambel (1957).

5. Mirambel (1951), (1951)[2].

6. Mirambel (1952).

7. Mirambel (1937).

8. The Chamber of Deputies until its dissolution in 1967 conducted its business in purist Greek. The few interventions in demotic made by General Sarafis, the former resistance leader, are said to have been electrifying in their effect.

9. Triantaphyllides (1949), Blanken (1956), Householder (1962).

10. Mirambel (1961)[2].

7

THE DIALECTS OF MODERN GREEK

The study of the dialects of modern Greek in the nineteenth century laboured under two difficulties, one of which has only partially been surmounted at the present day. The first was the absence of descriptive accounts of the speech of individual regions. Much has been done in more recent years to remedy this shortcoming, but much still remains to be done. There is still no linguistic atlas of Greece. There are still no descriptions of the dialect of many areas. And those which do exist are often based on antiquated principles, and take little account of modern linguistic science or of the advances that have been made in the study of the dialects of other European languages, particularly those of the Romance and Germanic families. The other shortcoming of earlier work in the field was the tendency to regard modern Greek dialects as the direct descendants of the dialects of ancient Greek. Scholars of the generation of F. W. Mullach sought to find Dorisms and Aeolisms in the medieval and modern Greek dialects, or even went further back, seeking the origin of certain of their characteristics in primitive Indo-European. We have seen that the ancient dialects were almost entirely replaced in late Hellenistic times by the Koine, the common Greek language based upon Attic. And it is clear that the dialects of modern Greek are all, with certain qualifications to be discussed later, the result of dialect differentiation within this common language, to which the ancient dialects, in so far as they survived at all, contributed extremely little.[1]

The evidence for the history and development of the dialects of medieval and modern Greek consists in the first place of the dialects as spoken today, secondly of such dialect differences as can be discerned in earlier vernacular Greek literature, and thirdly of references to dialect differences in the writings of grammarians and others in the middle ages and early modern times. Only when this evidence has been sifted can we go on to link the groups of the modern dialects with the political and demographic history of the Greek people. And the conclusions which we reach will necessarily be provisional and speculative.

Throughout mainland Greece, its offshore islands, the islands of the Aegean, and many of the coastal areas of Asia Minor and in Constantinople there were spoken until 1922–23 a group of dialects showing a great number of common features. The Greek population of the Asia Minor coast is now reduced to a small enclave in Smyrna, and that of Constantinople is very much reduced in numbers since the Asia Minor disaster. These dialects, and in particular those of the Peloponnese, formed the basis of the common spoken language of the present day, demotic Greek, as has been explained in an earlier chapter. Within the area in which they are spoken there run a number of lines of cleavage – isoglosses – some of which have been used by linguists as a basis of classification of the dialects. The lines of cleavage do not coincide with one another, and no single one is a sufficient basis for classification. Hence classificatory schemes have varied very much. In fact until we have sufficient material collected in the field in accordance with the principles of modern dialect study, it is probably best to leave the question of ultimate classification open.[2]

The most striking of the lines of cleavage is concerned with the treatment of unaccented vowels. North and east of a line which runs down the coast of Epirus and Acarnania, then along the Gulf of Corinth, across the Isthmus, along the northern mountain frontier of Attica, south of Euboea, through the middle of the island of Andros, north of Icaria and south of Samos, and so to the coast of Asia Minor, leaving to the west and south the Ionian islands, the whole of the Peloponnese, Attica, and most of the Cyclades, unaccented *i* and *u* vanish, unaccented *e* and *o* become *i* and *u*, and only *a* remains unchanged in unaccented position; accented vowels are not affected. Thus to common Greek χαιρέτησα 'I greeted' there corresponds northern χιρέτσα, to ἐλεύθερου, ἰλεύθερ and so on. The effect of this feature on the phonological and morphological structure of the northern dialects is far-reaching. The only final consonants permitted in the southern dialects are -s and -n, the latter being preserved only in certain phonetic conditions (see p. 79). In the northern dialects any consonant and a great many consonant groups can occur in final position. Many consonantal combinations occur in the northern dialects which are not permissible in the southern dialects and common Greek. Patterns of noun declension and verb conjugation change radically, as will be seen from the following examples:

Southern and common	Northern
ἄνθρωπος 'man'	ἄνθρουπους
ἄνθρωπο	ἄνθρουπου
ἀνθρώπου	ἀνθρώπ
ἄνθρωποι or ἀνθρώποι	ἄνθρουπ or ἀνθρώπ
ἀνθρώπους	ἀνθρώπς
ἀνθρώπω(ν)	ἀνθρώπου(ν)
μύτη 'nose'	μύτ
μύτη	μύτ
μύτης	μύτς
μύτες	μύτις
μύτες	μύτις
μυτῶ(ν)	μτω(ν)
λείπω 'leave'	λείπου
λείπεις	λείπς
λείπει	λείπ
λείπομε(ν)	λείπουμι(ν)
λείπετε	λείπιτι
λείπουν	λείπν(ι)
μεσημέρι 'midday'	μισμέρ
παιδεύω 'punish'	πιδεύου
παίδεψα	παίδιψα
παιδεύομαι	πιδεύουμι
παιδεύτηκα	πιδεύτκα
σπίτι 'house'	σπίτ
σπιτιού	σπτιοῦ
γλεντίζει 'celebrates'	γλιντίζ
γλέντισε	γλέντσι
περιμένει 'waits'	πιρμέν
περίμενε	πιρίμινι etc.

The other lines of cleavage which divide the main bloc of mainland and Aegean Greek dialects are less striking in their overall effect, but may none the less turn out to be more important for the purpose of classification. One which has attracted much attention concerns the presence of an irrational spirant between two adjacent vowels. In many regions of mainland Greece this occurs between vowels but not between vowel plus v and vowel, e.g. κλαίγω but δουλεύω. In the Sporades and parts of the Peloponnese it does not occur between vowels, but does between vowel plus v and following vowel, e.g. κλαίω but δουλεύγω. In most of the Cyclades, Lesbos, Icaria and Crete it occurs in both situations, e.g. κλαίγω, δουλεύγω. Another line of cleavage divides those regions where a nasal is preserved before a following occlusive and those where it is lost. In most of mainland Greece, in the islands of Zakynthos and Kythera, in Chios and in the Dodecanese one says ἄντρας, in Thrace, southern Macedonia, eastern Thessaly, northern Euboea, and in the Cyclades and Crete one says ἄδρας. Other lines of cleavage in matters of phonetics concern the pronunciation of the group -ία with or without synizezis, the palatalisation of χ to š and of κ to č before i and e. At a different level there is a line of cleavage regarding the position of the object pronoun: in most parts of Greece the order is τὸν ἄκουσα but in some regions it is ἄκουσά τον. A more important syntactic line of cleavage is that which runs down the ridge of Mount Pindus, south of Thessaly, south of the Sporades and of Lesbos. North and east of this line the indirect object of a verb is in the accusative, e.g. σὲ δίνω; in the rest of Greece, and in common demotic, it is in the dative, e.g. σοῦ δίνω.

Eastwards, southwards and westwards of this main bloc of dialects there stretches a belt of archaic dialects, all of which share some of a number of characteristics not found in the main bloc. These dialects comprise Bithynian, Pontic, in north-eastern Asia Minor, and with an outlier in the region of Rostov in southern Russia (since 1922–23 Pontic is no longer spoken in Asia Minor, and knowledge of it is rapidly disappearing among the descendants of the refugees settled in various parts of Greece), the strange Greek of Mariupol, the dialects of the interior of Asia Minor, spoken in three separate enclaves (Cappodocia and the two smaller regions of Phárasa and Sílli) before 1922–23, the dialect of Livisi in the south-west corner of Asia Minor before 1922–23, Cypriot, the Dodecanesian dialects, and the dialects of the two surviving Greek enclaves in southern Italy, in a group of villages south of Lecce in Apulia and around Bova in Calabria. Features which some or all of these dialects share are the pronunciation of double consonants where these occurred in classical Greek, e.g. ἄλ-λος, 'Ελ-λάδα; the preservation of final -ν, the preservation of an accusative plural in -ας opposed to the nominative in -ες: third person plural of verbs in -ουσι and -ασι instead of -ουν and -αν. In addition they preserve many lexical elements which have been lost or replaced in the main bloc of dialects and hence in demotic.[3] Some of the Asia Minor dialects often, but not always, represent koine η by ε, thus νύφε, πολίτες. And the system of aspects of the verb is organised in a structure different from that of 'normal' Greek. The Italian dialects show loss of final -ς, preservation of infinitive and participles, and sometimes -α- representing common Greek -η- from proto-Hellenic -ᾱ-, i.e. they apparently preserve a trace of Doric, or at any rate non-Attic phonology. There are traces of this non-Attic α in Cretan, and here and there elsewhere, but only in isolated words, in particular in place-names, which are particularly stable in form.

Finally there is the very aberrant Tsakonian dialect spoken in a mountainous area on the east coast of the Peloponnese, and in a slightly different form, until 1922–23, on the south coast of the Sea of Marmara.[4] Tsakonian shows many features which link it with the latest recorded form of the Laconian dialect of ancient Sparta, e.g. retention of α in place of common Greek η, e.g. τὰν ἀμέρα, ἀ μάτη (=ἡ μήτηρ); pronunciation of original υ as ου, e.g. γουναῖκα, κουβάνε (κυάνεος), κούνε (κύων); representation of an original digamma – which survived longest in the Doric dialects of the Peloponnese – by β, e.g. δαβελέ (cf. Hesych. δαβελός δαλός) βάννε (ἄρνος); rhotacism of originally final -ς, e.g. τᾶρ ἀμερί (τῆς ἡμέρας), νὰ χαρῆρε (νὰ χαρῆς); representation of original θ by σ, e.g. σέρι (θέρος); loss of intervocalic -σ-, e.g. ὁροῦα (ὁρῶσα). It also preserves many words not surviving elsewhere in spoken Greek, e.g. ἄντε (ἄρτος), ὄνε (ὄνος), ἐκιοῦ (τύ – σύ), ὔο (ὕδωρ); note in the last word the treatment of upsilon; it cannot be a recent borrowing from some other dialect, for it is unknown in other dialects, where it is replaced by νερό, yet it shows the common Greek rendering i, and not the Doric u. In fact Tsakonian looks like the descendant of a late form of Peloponnesian Doric already heavily contaminated by Koine. This dialect is also extremely aberrant in its verbal conjugation. The present stem forms no indicative tenses, the present and imperfect indicative being formed by a periphrasis

with 'to be' and the present participle – cf. the Hellenistic ἦν
διδασκων – thus we have:

	Masc.	Fem.	Neut.
Present	ἔμι ὀροῦ	ὀροῦα	ὀροῦντα
	ἔσσι ὀροῦ	ὀροῦα	ὀροῦντα
	ἔννι ὀροῦ	ὀροῦα	ὀροῦντα
	ἔμμε ὀροῦντε		
	ἔττε ὀροῦντε		
	εἶσι ὀροῦντε		
Imperfect	ἔμα ὀροῦ	ὀροῦα	ὀροῦντα
	ἔσα ὀροῦ	ὀροῦα	ὀροῦντα
	ἔκη ὀροῦ	ὀροῦα	ὀροῦντα
	ἔμαϊ ὀροῦντε		
	ἔτταϊ ὀροῦντε		
	ἤγκη ὀροῦντε		

The implications of this verb pattern for the structure of
Tsakonian as compared with other Greek dialects will be considered later in this chapter. The Tsakonian of Asia Minor,
spoken by the descendants of settlers from the eastern Peloponnese in the fifteenth century, has a similarly organised verbal
conjugation.

Of vernacular or near-vernacular literary texts the earliest
show no significant coincidence with any of the modern dialects.
Cypriot, with many of its present characteristics, is found recorded
as early as the fourteenth century in the Assizes of Cyprus, in
the fifteenth century in the Chronicle of Leontios Machairas,
early in the sixteenth century in that of George Boustronios,
and in a collection of love poems in a sixteenth-century manuscript now in the Marcian Library in Venice.[5] Cretan poetry of
the sixteenth century shows many dialect features, and that of
the seventeenth century is largely in a standardised language based
upon the spoken dialects of eastern Crete.[6] Otherwise there is
little in the way of recognisable dialect texts until the nineteenth
century. Certain Greek texts written in Hebrew characters for
the use of Greek-speaking Jewish communities in the twelfth–
thirteenth centuries and the sixteenth century respectively have
been held to show identifying traits of this or that dialect. But
their orthography is so imprecise that few conclusions can be
drawn from them.[7] A fifteenth-century Russian–Greek phrase
book shows typical features of the present day northern dialects.[8]

The remarks of medieval and early modern Greek grammarians on local varieties of Greek spoken in their own time are in general vitiated by the conception that the ancient Greek dialects still existed. For instance, Kabasilas writes (Crusius, *Turco-graecia*, 461): Περὶ δὲ τῶν διαλέκτων τί ἂν καὶ εἴποιμι, πολλῶν οὐσῶν καὶ διαφόρων ὑπὲρ τὰς ἑβδομήκοντα . . . ἔτι τῶν ἡμετέρων ἰδιωτῶν τοὺς μὲν Δωρικῶς, τους δὲ ᾿Αττικῶς, ἄλλους Αἰολικῶς, ἑτέρους ᾿Ιωνικῶς, πρὸς δὲ τούτοις κοινῶς φθεγγομένους εὑρήσει τις 'Of the dialects what am I to say, since they are many and varied, more than seventy in number . . . furthermore of our uneducated people you will find some speaking Doric, some Attic, others Aeolic, others Ionic, and yet others the common tongue.' However, Eustathios, teacher in the Patriarchal School in Constantinople in the third quarter of the twelfth century and later Metropolitan of Thessalonica has some interesting observations in his extensive commentary on Homer, e.g. that some people in the east say ἀχάντια instead of ἀκάνθια, a feature characteristic of present-day Pontic (Eust 468.33). At the end of the twelfth century Michal Choniates, Metropolitan of Athens, cites words and forms typical of the Athenian dialect of his day (S. Lambros, Μιχαὴλ Χωνιάτου τὰ σωζόμενα II, Athens 1880, 43). The fifteenth-century satirical dialogue *Mazaris* mentions Tsakonian, but the examples which it cites are false.

Greek loan-words in neighbouring languages may sometimes furnish useful indications. There are, for instance, many Greek loan-words in the Aromunian of the transhumant Vlach shepherds of Epirus and Pindus. Their settlement in these regions took place between the eighth and tenth centuries, and they can be presumed to have been illiterate then, as they were until the twentieth century, and to have had little or no contact with Greek literary culture. The fact that these loan-words do not show the treatment of unaccented vowels typical of the northern Greek dialects spoken in their area of settlement is good evidence that these changes had not taken place at the time of their settlement, and so provides a *terminus post quem*. Even in this case, however, caution is necessary. There are areas in Epirus at the present day in which the northern Greek vowel changes do not occur. But they are probably the result of later population movements. And in any case the likelihood that the nomad Vlachs borrowed all their Greek words from one or two small areas is slight. Greek loan-words in South Slavonic are of more doubtful evidential value, since many of them were made from

5

purist Greek by men of learning. But there are some oddities
which never seem to have been satisfactorily explained. What is
one to make, for instance, of Serbian *panadjur* (from πανήγυρις),
which not only preserves the non-Attic *a* in the second syllable,
as do some forms of the word in modern Greek, but also represents the upsilon of the third syllable by *u*? Early Russian loan-
words present some problems too, e.g. *korabl'* from καράβιον
with *beta* represented by *b* instead of the usual *v*. There is room
for a fresh study of all early Slavonic borrowings from Greek
by a competent Greek dialectologist.[9]

We may now turn to the history of the Greek dialects. Once
the Koine had become the speech of the vast majority of Greek
speakers from Sicily to the Iranian frontier, two tendencies
were continuously at work. On the one hand, there was the
natural tendency of a language spoken over a wide area to develop regional differences, which in the case of Greek may have
been strengthened by long periods of bilingualism in certain
areas and the consequent effects of the linguistic substratum on
the Greek spoken there. This would be particularly the case in
Asia Minor, the Hellenisation of which was a very slow process,
despite the early establishment of a large number of Greek cities
in the east and in the interior. On the other hand, there was the
unifying effect of the common literary language, of the frequent
and easy communication between the different parts of the empire, of the conscious efforts of schools to maintain conformity
to a standard, of the church, with its common language of liturgy
and predication, and all the factors making for uniformity in a
centralised state whose uniform institutions enjoyed great prestige. In the areas where Greek had been for centuries the language of the whole population, i.e. in mainland Greece, the
islands, the west coast of Asia Minor, and in Sicily and south
Italy the Koine spoken, especially in the remoter parts of the
countryside or among the members of any relatively closed
group, might still show strong traces of the ancient Greek dialect
of the region. What we must look for in trying to establish the
origin and early history of the modern dialects are situations in
which this or that area is to some degree cut off from the rest of
the Greek-speaking community, and the tendency towards uniformity thus weakened.

One such situation would be that created by the invasion and
partial settlement of the Peloponnese by the Avars and their
Slav subjects in the penultimate decade of the sixth century

(Evagr. *Hist. Eccl.* 6.10, *Chron. Monemvas.* pp. 65–70). Our sources speak of wholesale movements of population, and one source, a chronicle of great interest but uncertain reliability, speaks of migration of shepherds from Laconia to the mountainous region near Monemvasia, shepherds whose descendants were called Tsakonians. Whether this is genuine folk tradition or learned construction is a moot point. Be that as it may, there is no doubt that the Slavonic invasions forced many of the Greek population of the Peloponnese to withdraw into the least accessible and most easily defensible areas.[10] The wild mountains of Tsakonia are just such an area – those for whom a visit is impossible should read the interesting account of the area in the early sixties of last century by Gustave Deville in the introduction to his *Étude du dialecte Tzaconien*, Paris 1866. Most of the interior of the Peloponnese was effectively withdrawn from Byzantine control until the beginning of the ninth century, though Byzantine claims to sovereignty were never, of course, given up. Tzakonia, though on the coast, has no port, and a dangerous and forbidding coast-line; it must be counted as a part of the interior. We know that of all the ancient Greek dialects the Doric of the Peloponnese was that which survived longest on the lips of the peasantry. In the remoter areas of the Peloponnese it seems *a priori* likely that as late as the sixth century a very Dorising Koine, if not pure Doric, was spoken. For a couple of centuries the mountain dwellers of Tsakonia would be virtually cut off from the rest of the Greek-speaking community, and their dialect would develop in the absence of the tendencies to uniformity which prevailed elsewhere. It is to these circumstances that we must attribute the origin of the Tsakonian dialect, and its isolated position among the dialects of modern Greek, in being to some extent the descendant of one of the dialects of ancient Greek. The remoteness and inaccessibility of their homeland have until today prevented their dialect from replacement by one of the neighbouring dialects or by common demotic, though they have not prevented influences from these varieties of Greek affecting Tsakonian. The first mention of the Tsakonians is by Constantine Porphyrogenitus in the middle of the tenth century, who speaks of them as forming a special corps in the Byzantine army.[11] Their name is probably to be connected with that of the ancient Laconians, though the precise etymology is still disputed.

The invasions and settlement of the Seljuk Turks in the closing decades of the eleventh century put an end for ever to Byzantine power in most of the interior of Asia Minor. Areas were recovered and lost again, and considerable movements of population took place. The Greek church remained in being, giving some kind of cultural unity to the dwindling Greek communities, but in general the conditions favoured dialect differentiation and preservation of peculiarities rather than uniformity. Most of Pontus, it is true, was never effectively occupied by the Seljuks. But it was isolated from the rest of the Byzantine empire, was virtually independent during part of the twelfth century under the dynasts of the Gabras family, and from the beginning of the thirteenth century until the middle of the fifteenth it formed the independent Empire of Trebizond. The Pontic Greeks led a strange frontier life, fighting with the nomadic Turcomans for the high pastures of the Matzouka, and had little contact with the main areas of Greek settlement further west. The Seljuk invasion and the subsequent Ottoman occupation were certainly a major factor in the continuing differentiation between the Asia Minor dialects and those of the rest of the Hellenic world. Many have held that they provide a sufficient explanation of the present-day dialect situation. However, it is doubtful whether they provide sufficient time for the development of the distinguishing characteristics of the Asia Minor dialects. Already in the twelfth century Eustathios cites one characteristic Pontic form. Unfortunately we have virtually no evidence for the condition of the Asia Minor dialects from then until the early nineteenth century, so we cannot tell when they acquired their present shape. It seems probable that the Arab invasions of the seventh and eighth centuries, together with the local peculiarities of Koine Greek in Asia Minor, provided the conditions in which the speech of these areas began to be significantly differentiated from common spoken Koine. Cappadocia, where the largest of the Greek enclaves in Asia Minor was situated until 1922–23 was a frontier area in those crucial centuries, where Moslem and Christian frontiersmen maintained an uneasy peace punctuated by raids and reprisals. It was in Cappadocia that the independent Paulician state was set up in the ninth century.[12] We have thus a long period beginning in the middle of the seventh century when the Greeks of this region were to some extent isolated from their fellows. The same is true of Pontus, which from the late sixth century was subject to Persian and later Arab invasions, and was constantly menaced by the Iberian Lazes.

In 632 the Arab fleet, under the command of Abu Bakr, father-in-law of the Prophet, made its appearance off Citium, on the south coast of Cyprus, and made its first short raid on the island. In 647 the Caliph Moawiya captured Constantia, the capital of the island, and became master of Cyprus for a short time. From then on there were almost annual attacks, causing widespread destruction, and the abandonment of many of the cities, whose inhabitants took to the mountains. The annual tribute of the island was divided between the Byzantine emperor and the Caliph, who established a kind of *de facto* condominium. Many Arabs appear to have settled in the island. At the end of the seventh century, according to our meagre sources, the majority of the Christian population was transferred to the European coast of the Hellespont – an event still commemorated in the official titulature of the Archbishop of Cyprus – and remained there for some ten years before returning to the island. From then until its final liberation by Nicephorus Phocas in 964 the island was partly, and sometimes wholly, occupied by the Arabs, and many of the ancient cities remained unoccupied. These three centuries of partial Arab occupation, of abandonment of urban life, and of loss of contact with the Byzantine empire are probably the period in which the Cypriot dialect began to follow a different path of development from the Greek of more central areas. By its first appearance in literature in the fourteenth century most of its present-day features were already established.

The islands of the Dodecanese, like Cyprus, were for long in a kind of no-man's-land between Byzantium and the Arabs, and it was probably at this time that the main distinctive features of their dialects – which have much in common with Cypriot – became established. In addition some of the islands themselves, such as Carpathos, had long been backwaters, out of the main stream of life in the late Roman and early Byzantine empire, important neither for war nor for trade nor for the tribute which they furnished. No doubt the Koine Greek spoken there before the advent of the Arabs had an odd and archaic colouring, and it may have preserved many features, though not whole structures, inherited from the dialect spoken there before the spread of Koine.

The Arab occupation of Crete was later and shorter than that of Cyprus. The island was seized by Arab emigrants from Spain, who had briefly settled in Egypt, in either 823 or 825, and it remained in Arab hands until its recapture by Nicephorus Phocas in 967. We know very little about the life of the Greek

population in Arab Crete. But there was certainly very little
intercourse with the rest of the Greek world.[13] This period of
occupation was probably crucial in establishing the differential
characteristics of the Cretan dialect, which is much less archaic
than those of Cyprus or the Dodecanese. No doubt even before
823 the speech of Crete, which played little part in the life of the
Byzantine empire, had begun to develop features of its own.

There are now only two tiny enclaves of Greek speech in
southern Italy. A few centuries ago their extent was much greater.
Still earlier one hears of Greek being currently spoken in many
parts of south Italy. Now it is clear that there was a considerable
immigration from Greece during Byzantine times. We hear of
refugees from the rule of the iconoclast emperors of the eighth
century – mostly monks and so unlikely to contribute permanently to the demographic pattern – as well as of fugitives from
the western Peloponnese and elsewhere during the Avar and Slav
invasions of the late sixth and seventh centuries. And during
the Byzantine reconquest of the late ninth and tenth centuries
there was a good deal of settlement by Greeks from other regions
of the empire on lands taken from the Arabs, or occasionally
from the Lombards. Students of Italian Greek in the nineteenth
century supposed that the surviving enclaves were the descendants of settlements made in Byzantine times, and looked –
more often than not in vain – for parallels in the dialects of
mainland Greece to the peculiar features of the Greek of Bova
and Otranto. It is now clear, above all from the researches of
Rohlfs and Caratzas,[14] that the speech of these enclaves is the
descendant, not of the language of Byzantine immigrants, but
of the Greek colonists of Magna Graecia. In other words Greek
never died out entirely in south Italy, though the area in which
it was spoken was greatly reduced by the advance of Latin. When
the Byzantine immigrants arrived they found a Greek-speaking
peasantry still settled on the land in some areas, whose speech
was an independent development of the vernacular of Magna
Graecia in the Late Roman Empire, no doubt a regional variety
of Koine with a heavy dialect colouring. Only by this hypothesis
can the presence of so many archaic features not found in any
other Greek dialect be explained. And there is nothing inconsis-
tent with it in the meagre historical record. Here then we have
a Greek-speaking community isolated from the rest of the Hellenic world virtually since the death of Theodosius in 395, with
a brief reintegration between Justinian's reconquest and the

growth of Lombard and Arab power, and again during the
Byzantine reoccupation in the tenth and eleventh centuries, and
always remote from the centres of power and culture. These
were the conditions which gave rise to the archaic and aberrant
Greek dialects of the now bilingual inhabitants of the two enclaves in the toe and the heel of Italy.

It is more difficult to determine the circumstances in which
the differences within the mainland group of dialects became
established. The peculiar treatment of unaccented vowels in the
northern dialects has been connected with the extensive Albanian
settlements in northern Greece in the later middle ages. But apart
from the fact that there is no similar feature in Albanian, recent
studies have suggested that there was no distinction between
accented and unaccented vowels in northern Greek before the
tenth century, and that the distinction was well established by
the twelfth; the Albanian immigration did not become massive
until the fourteenth century.[15] Slavonic influence is a possible
explanation, since considerable areas of northern Greece were
occupied for periods by the Bulgarians, and in certain Bulgarian
dialects today there is a similar differentiation between accented
and unaccented vowels. Other causes suggested are the influence
of a strong stress accent, and a continuation of a tendency to
narrow certain vowels which is already seen in the Thessalian
dialect of ancient Greek. A similar, but not identical, distinction
in treatment between accented and unaccented vowels is found
in some Asia Minor dialects, where it is probably of quite independent origin. What is certain is that the long Latin occupation
of most of mainland Greece and many of the Cyclades encouraged
dialectal differentiation, since the prestige of metropolitan speech
was lowered, and the traditional educational system largely
discontinued.[16] The lines followed by certain isoglosses today
are the result of population movements in the Turkish period.
For instance, the northern character of the dialect of Samos is
due to the settlement there of many immigrants from the northern
Greek mainland.

Greek communities settled outside Greece in modern times
have not generally developed a dialect of their own, but speak
common demotic, with more or less heavy lexical borrowings
from the language of the local population. This was true of the
large Greek community of Odessa before 1917, which had always
close links with Constantinople, of the even larger Greek communities of Alexandria and Cairo, and of other smaller settlements

in many parts of the world. The Greek communities in the United States tend to become assimilated and to lose their language. A recent study of the Greek community of Chicago has thrown an interesting light on the gradual anglicisation of the Greek of the bilingual generations, as well as on the tendency to reserve Greek for a more and more restricted group of situations.[17] The Cypriot Greek community of London, which is of very recent origin, is peculiar in that it consists of speakers of a single dialect or group of closely related dialects. The second generation is often bilingual in Cypriot Greek and English, with only an imperfect or passive knowledge of common demotic. The inhabitants of the Corsican village of Cargese speak – or rather spoke, since there are by now only a few old persons who have any facility in Greek – a Peloponnesian dialect, being descendants of immigrants from the western Peloponnese in the eighteenth century.[18] It is not clear to the present writer to what extent the Pontic dialect of Rostov and the very strange dialect of Mariupol still survive. The Soviet census of 1959 recorded 309,300 persons of Greek 'nationality', but this does not necessarily imply that they all speak Greek as their first or second language.[19]

As has already been indicated, there are considerable structural differences between certain of the dialects and common demotic. On the level of phonology, common demotic, and the southern dialects of the mainland and those of the southern Cyclades and Crete, together with those of the Dodecanese and Cyprus, have a triangular system of five vowel phonemes, while the northern dialects have a similar system of five phonemes in accented syllables, but a three-phoneme system in unaccented syllables. The dialect of Phárasa in Asia Minor has a six-vowel system in accented syllables, and the normal five-vowel system in unaccented syllables. Pontic, together with the Tsakonian of the Propontis and certain dialects of Thrace and Thessaly show a seven-vowel system in all syllables. Cappadocian and the dialect of Sílli have a quadrangular system of eight vowel phonemes, which is that of the surrounding Turkish. In these dialects a series of new noun-types has arisen parallel to those in *a, e, i, o* and *u* of common demotic. The development of vocalic harmony of the Turkish pattern in the dialects of Cappadocia and Sílli has led to the creation of a double series of terminations in the present of verbs with terminal accentuation: eu, -as, -a, -umi, -ati, -uši, and -o, -es, -e, -ümi, -ete, -üši.[20]

While in common demotic, and the dialects of the mainland

and the islands, all verbs have two themes, each of which forms one or more indicative tenses, a future tense, a subjunctive and a conditional, this regular pattern is subject to considerable perturbation in Tsakonian and in the Asia Minor dialects.[21] In Tsakonian only the aorist theme can form an indicative tense, though both themes form subjunctive and futures. The present and imperfect indicative are formed by periphrases with a present participle, akin to the English 'I am going', thus the symmetry between the themes is broken. The dialects of Cappadocia and Sílli have two verbal themes, but only the aorist theme is capable of producing a subjunctive and a future. There is thus no opposition of aspect in the subjunctive and the future, as there is in common demotic. The same structure is found in the dialect of Phárasa, and in addition there is no perfect tense, its functions having been taken over by the aorist. The Pontic dialects also limit the expression of aspect to the indicative, though the details vary, some dialects preserving the present subjunctive, others the aorist. How far these divergences from the common Greek verbal pattern are due to Turkish influence is a matter of speculation, since we have no texts in these dialects from an early period.

Some of the Asia Minor dialects, together with the Greek of Mariupol, the speakers of which are descended from settlers from the Crimea, show a rearrangement of the system of genders, resulting in a differentiation between animate and inanimate substantives. This is often accompanied by a reduction in the use of the article, and consequent weakening of the distinction between definite and indefinite substantives. These features are probably due to Turkish or Tatar influence, since these communities were largely bilingual. Mariupol Greek has in addition lost the genitive case entirely, and expresses possession by a construction modelled on that of Tatar, e.g. *spiti-t porta* (the door of the house), *tata-t tu spit* (his father's house).[22]

It is thus clear that behind the impressive variety of Greek dialects over a great area, a unity fostered by cultural factors, above all the influence of education, there are very varied structural patterns, which in the absence of these cultural factors could have given rise to a group of languages at least as divergent as those of the Romance or the Slavonic family.

---

1. Mirambel (1953); Pop (1950); Kapsomenos (1958), 16–31, where further bibliographical indications will be found.

2. On the problem of classification cf. the above works, and also Triantaphyllidis (1938) 62–74; Dawkins (1940).

3. The concept of a fringe of archaic dialects with certain archaic features in common which were lost by the central dialects is discussed, with full references to the literature, by Caratzas (1958).

4. Pernot (1934); Kostakis (1951).

5. Ed. Siapkaras-Pitsillides (1952).

6. Embiricos (1960); Manoussacas (1953).

7. Hesseling (1901), (1897); Perles (1893).

8. Vasmer (1923).

9. The basic collection of material is still Vasmer (1900), (1907), (1909).

10. Bon (1951) 27–74.

11. Constantine Porphyrogenitus, *De caerimoniis* (ii, 49).

12. cf. Garsoian (1967), where references to the relevant literature will be found.

13. Embiricos (1960) 31; Papadopoulos (1948).

14. cf. the list of Rohlfs' works on South-Italian Greek on p. 145 in the bibliography. For the references to Caratzas cf. note 3.

15. Andriotis (1933).

16. Anagnostopoulos (1924).

17. Seaman (1965).

18. Blanken (1951).

19. There are still Greek-speaking communities in Abkhazia and in Southern Georgia (Letter of Dr Irina Nodia, Georgian Academy of Sciences, of 21 May 1969).

20. Mirambel (1965).

21. Mirambel (1964).

22. The only adequate descriptive study of Mariupol Greek is Sergievskij (1934).

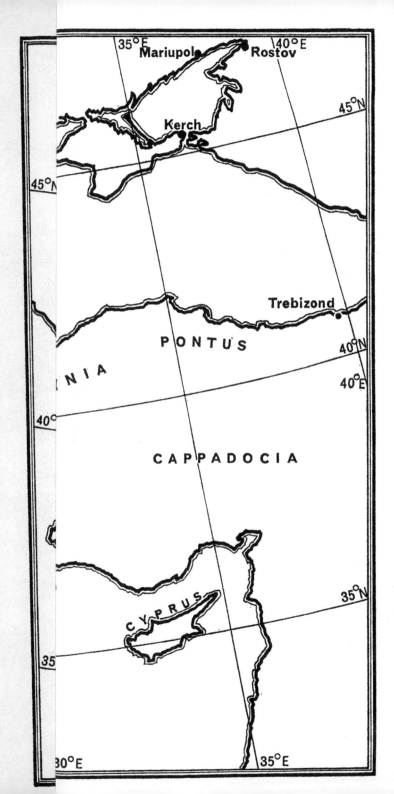

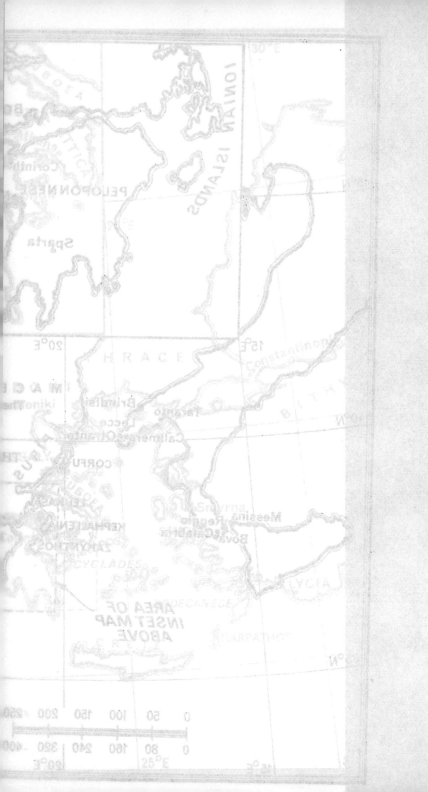

BIBLIOGRAPHY

AERTS (1965)
W. J. Aerts, *Periphrastica. An investigation into the use of* εἶναι *and* ἔχειν *as auxiliaries or pseudo-auxiliaries in Greek from Homer up to the present day*, Amsterdam, 1965.

ALESSIO DA SOMAVERA (1709)
Alessio da Somavera, *Tesoro della lingua greca volgare ed italiana*, Paris, 1709.

ANAGNOSTOPOULOS (1922)
G. P. Anagnostopoulos, *Ἀθηνᾶ* 34 (1922) 166–247.

ANAGNOSTOPOULOS (1924)
G. P. Anagnostopoulos, Εἰσαγωγὴ εἰς τὴν νεοελληνικὴν φιλολογίαν. Α. Περί τῆς ἀρχῆς τῶν νέων Ἑλληνικῶν διαλέκτων, Ἐπετηρὶς Ἑταιρείας Βυζαντινῶν Σπουδῶν 1 (1924) 93–108.

ANDRIOTIS (1933)
N. P. Andriotis, Περί τῆς ἀρχῆς τῶν Βορείων γλωσσικῶν ἰδιωμάτων τῆς νέας Ἑλληνικῆς, Ἐπετηρὶς Ἑταιρείας Βυζαντινῶν Σπουδῶν 10 (1933) 340–352.

ANDRIOTIS (1948)
N. P. Andriotis, Τὸ γλωσσικὸ ἰδίωμα τῶν Φαράσων, Athens, 1948.

ANDRIOTIS (1961)
N. P. Andriotis (1961) Τὸ ἰδίωμα τοῦ Λιβισιοῦ τῆς Λυκίας, Athens, 1961.

ANLAUF (1960)
G. Anlauf, *Standard Late Greek oder Attizismus. Eine Studie zum Optativgebrauch im nachklassischen Griechisch*, Cologne, 1960.

ANTONIADIS (1939)
S. Antoniadis, *La place de la liturgie dans la tradition des lettres grecques*, Leiden, 1939.

ATKINSON (1936)
B. F. C. Atkinson, *The Greek Language*, London, 1936.

BACHTIN (1935)
N. Bachtin, *Introduction to the study of Modern Greek*, Cambridge, 1935.

BĂNESCU (1915)
N. Bănescu, *Die Entwicklung des griechischen Futurums von der frühbyzantinischen Zeit bis zur Gegenwart*, Bucharest, 1915.

BATTISTI (1950)
C. Battisti, *Avviamento allo studio del latino volgare*, Bari, 1950.

BEAUDOIN (1883)
N. Beaudouin, *Étude du dialecte chypriote moderne et médiéval*, Paris, 1883.

BEŠEVLIEV (1963)
V. Beševliev, *Die protobulgarischen Inschriften*, Berlin, 1963.

BJÖRCK (1940)
G. Björck, *Ἦν διδάσκων. Die periphrastischen Konstruktionen im Griechischen*, Uppsala, 1940.

BLACK (1954)
M. Black, *An Aramaic Approach to the Gospels and Acts*, 2nd ed. Oxford, 1954.

BLANKEN (1947)
G. H. Blanken, *Introduction à une étude du dialecte grec de Cargèse, Corse. Préliminaires. Phonétique*, Leiden, 1947.

BLANKEN (1951)
G. H. Blanken, *Les Grecs de Cargèse, Corse. Recherches sur leur langue et sur leur histoire*, Leiden, 1951.

BLANKEN (1956)
G. H. Blanken, 'De taalkwestie in hedendags Griekenland', *Mededelingen van de Koninklijke Vlaamse Academie voor Wetenschappen, Letteren en Schone Kunsten van België*, Kl. der Letteren 18 (1956), no. 6.

BLASS-DEBRUNNER (1961)
F. Blass, *Grammatik des neutestamentlichen Griechisch*. Bearb. von A. Debrunner, 11. Aufl., Göttingen, 1961.

BOARDMAN (1964)
J. Boardman, *The Greeks Overseas*, Harmondsworth, 1964.

BÖHLIG (1957)
G. Böhlig, 'Das Verhältnis von Volkssprache und Reinsprache im griechischen Mittelalter', *Aus der byzantinischen Arbeit der Deutschen Demokratischen Republik*, Berlin, 1957, 1–13.

BON (1951)
A. Bon, *Le Péloponnèse byzantin jusqu'en 1204*, Paris, 1951.

BUCHNER AND RUSSO (1955)
G. Buchner and C. F. Russo, 'La coppa di Nestore e un iscrizione metrica da Pitecusa dell'VIII secolo av. Cr.', *Rendiconti dell'Accademia dei Lincei*, N.S. 10 (1955) 215–234.

BUCK AND PETERSEN (1945)
C. D. Buck and W. Petersen, *A Reverse Index of Greek Nouns and Adjectives*, Chicago, 1945.

CAMERON (1931)
A. Cameron, 'Latin words in the Greek inscriptions of Asia Minor', *American Journal of Philology* 52 (1931) 232–262.

CARATZAS (1958)[1]
S. Caratzas, *L'origine des dialectes néo-grecs de l'Italie méridionale*, Paris, 1958.

CARATZAS (1958)[2]
S. C. Caratzas, 'Die Entstehung der neugriechischen Literatursprache', *Glotta* 36 (1958) 194–208.

CASKEY (1965)
J. L. Caskey, 'Greece, Crete and the Aegean Islands in the Early Bronze Age' (*Cambridge Ancient History*, new ed.), Cambridge, 1965.

CHADWICK (1958)
J. Chadwick, *The Decipherment of Linear B*, Cambridge, 1958.

CHADWICK (1963)
J. Chadwick, 'The Prehistory of the Greek Language' (*Cambridge Ancient History*, new ed.), Cambridge, 1963.

CHANTRAINE (1927)
P. Chantraine, *Histoire du parfait grec*, Paris, 1927.

CHARANIS (1959)
P. Charanis, 'Ethnic Changes in the Byzantine Empire in the Seventh Century', *Dumbarton Oaks Papers* 13 (1959) 22–44.

CHATZIDAKIS (1892)
G. N. Chatzidakis, *Einleitung in die neugriechische Grammatik*, Leipzig, 1892.

CHATZIDAKIS (1905)
G. N. Chatzidakis, Μεσαιωνικὰ καὶ Νέα ῾Ελληνικά, 2 vols, Athens, 1905.

CHATZIDAKIS (1915)
G. N. Chatzidakis, Σύντομος ἱστορία τῆς νεοελληνικῆς γλώσσης, Athens, 1915.

CHATZIDAKIS (1930)
G. N. Chatzidakis, Περὶ τῆς διαιρέσεως τῆς ἱστορίας τῆς ἑλληνικῆς γλώσσης εἰς διαφόρους περιόδους, ᾿Επετηρὶς ῾Εταιρείας Βυζαντινῶν Σπουδῶν, 7 (1930) 227–230.

COSTAS (1936)
P. S. Costas, An outline of the history of the Greek language, with particular emphasis on the Koine and the subsequent periods, Chicago, 1936.

DANGUITSIS (1943)
C. Danguitsis, Étude descriptive du dialecte de Demirdesi, Brousse, Paris, 1943.

DAWKINS (1916)
R. M. Dawkins, Modern Greek in Asia Minor, Cambridge, 1916.

DAWKINS (1932)
R. M. Dawkins, 'Study of the Modern Greek of Pontos', Byzantion 6 (1932) 389 ff.

DAWKINS (1937)
R. M. Dawkins, 'The Pontic Dialect of Modern Greek in Asia Minor and Russia', Transactions of the Philological Society (1937) 15–52.

DAWKINS (1940)
R. M. Dawkins, 'The Dialects of Modern Greek', Transactions of the Philological Society (1940) 1–38.

DEBRUNNER (1954)
A. Debrunner, Geschichte der Griechischen Sprache, II: Grundfragen und Grundzüge des nachklassischen Griechisch, Berlin, 1954.

DIETERICH (1898)
K. Dieterich, Untersuchungen zur Geschichte der griechischen Sprache von der hellenistischen Zeit bis zum 10. Jahrhundert nach Christo, Leipzig, 1898.

DIMARAS (1967)
D. Dimaras, Histoire de la littérature grecque moderne, 2 vols, Paris, 1967.

DIRINGER (1968)
D. Diringer, The Alphabet, 3rd ed., London, 1968.

DÖLGER (1952)
F. Dölger, *Ein Fall slavischer Einsiedlung im Hinterland von Thessalonike im 10. Jahrhundert*, Munich, 1952.

DRESSLER (1966)
W. Dressler, 'Von Altgriechischen zum Neugriechischen System der Personalpronomina', *Indogermanische Forschungen* 71 (1966) 39–63.

EMBIRICOS (1960)
A. Embiricos, *La renaissance crétoise*, Paris, 1960.

FABRICIUS (1962)
C. Fabricius. *Zu den Jugendschriften des Johannes Chrysostomos Untersuchungen zum Klassizismus des vierten Jahrhunderts*, Lund, 1962.

FABRICIUS (1967)
C. Fabricius, Der Sprachliche Klassizismus der griechischen Kirchenväter. Ein philologisches und geistesgeschichtliches Problem. *Jahrbuch für Antike und Christentum* (1967).

GARSOIAN (1967)
N. G. Garsoian, *The Paulician Heresy. A Study of the Origin and Development of Paulicianism in Armenia and the eastern Provinces of the Byzantine Empire*, The Hague–Paris, 1967.

GEORGE AND MILLERSON (1966–7)
V. George and C. Millerson, 'The Cypriot Community in London', *Race* 8 (1966–7) 277–292.

GHEDINI (1937)
G. Ghedini, 'La lingua dei vangeli apocrifi greci', *Studi dedicati alla memoria di P. Ubaldi*, Milan, 1937, 443–480.

HAVRÁNEK (1966)
B. Havránek, *Travaux linguistiques de Prague* 2 (1966) 81–95.

HENRY (1943)
R. de L. Henry, *The Late Greek Optative and its Use in the Writings of Gregory Nazianzen*, Washington, 1943.

HESSELING (1897)
D. C. Hesseling, *Les cinq livres de la loi (la Pentateuque)*, Leipzig, 1897.

HESSELING (1901)
D. C. Hesseling, 'Le livre de Jonas', *Byzantinische Zeitschrift* 10 (1901) 208–217.

HESSELING AND PERNOT (1913)
D. C. Hesseling and H. Pernot, *Chansons d'amour* Paris, 1913.

HIGGINS (1945)
M. J. Higgins, 'The Renaissance of the First Century and the Origin of Standard Late Greek', *Traditio* 3 (1945) 49–100.

HØEG (1925–26)
C. Høeg, *Les Saracatsans*, 2 vols, Paris, 1925–26.

HOUSEHOLDER (1962)
F. W. Householder, 'Greek Diglossia', *Georgetown University Monograph series on Languages and Linguistics*, no. 15 (1962) 109–129.

HUMBERT (1930)
J. Humbert, *La disparition du datif en grec du Ier au Xe siècle*, Paris, 1930.

IRMSCHER (1956)
Ἰάκωβος Τριβώλης, Ποιήματα, herausgegeben von J. Irmscher, Berlin, 1956.

JANNARIS (1897)
A. N. Jannaris, *An Historical Greek Grammar, chiefly of the Attic Dialect*, Oxford, 1897.

JEFFERY (1961)
L. H. Jeffery, *The Local Scripts of Archaic Greece*, Oxford, 1961.

KAHANE AND TIETZE (1958)
H. and R. Kahane and A. Tietze, *The Lingua Franca in the Levant*, Urbana, Illinois, 1958.

KAPSOMENOS (1953)
S. Kapsomenos, Συμβολὴ στὴν ἱστορία τοῦ ῥήματος εἰμί, Προσφορὰ εἰς Σ. Κυριακίδην, Thessalonika, 1953, 305 ff.

KAPSOMENOS (1958)
S. Kapsomenos, Die griechische Sprache zwischen Koine und Neugriechisch. *Berichte zum XI. Internationalen Byzantinisten–Kongress*, München, 1958.

KESISOGLU (1951)
I. Kesisoglu, Τὸ γλωσσικὸ ἰδίωμα τοῦ Οὐλαγάτς, Athens, 1951.

KNÖS (1962)
B. Knös, *Histoire de la littérature néogrecque* I, Stockholm, 1962.

KORDATOS (1943)
I. Kordatos, Ἱστορία τοῦ γλωσσικοῦ μας ζητήματος, Athens, 1943.

KOSTAKIS (1951)
A. Kostakis, Σύντομη γραμματικὴ τῆς Τσακωνικῆς διαλέκτου, Athens, 1951.

KRETSCHMER (1905)
P. Kretschmer, *Der heutige lesbische Dialekt verglichen mit den übrigen nordgriechischen Mundarten*, Vienna, 1905.

LEGRAND (1874)
E. Legrand, *Collection des monuments pour servir à l'étude de la langue néo-hellénique*, nouvelle série, 2, Paris, 1874.

LEGRAND (1918)
E. Legrand, *Bibliographie hellénique, ou description raisonnée des ouvrages publiés par des Grecs au dix-huitième siècle* I, Paris, 1918.

LEJEUNE (1966)
M. Lejeune, 'La diffusion de l'alphabet', *Comptes Rendus de l'Académie des Inscriptions et Belles Lettres* (1966) 505–511.

LINNÉR (1943)
S. Linnér, *Syntaktische und lexikalische Studien zur Historia Lausiaca des Palladios*, Uppsala, 1943.

LJUNGVIK (1926)
H. Ljungvik, *Studien zur Sprache der apokryphen Apostelgeschichten*, Uppsala, 1926.

LJUNGVIK (1932)
H. Ljungvik, *Beiträge zur Syntax der spätgriechischen Volkssprache*, Uppsala, 1932.

MAAS (1912)
P. Maas, 'Metrische Akklamationen der Byzantiner', *Byzantinische Zeitschrift* 21 (1912) 28–51.

MAGIE (1905)
D. Magie, *De Romanorum iuris publici sacrique vocabulis sollemnibus in graecum sermonem conversis*, Leipzig, 1905.

MANOUSSAKAS (1953)
M. Manoussakas, *Κριτικὴ βιβλιογραφία τοῦ Κρητικοῦ Θεάτρου*, Ἑλληνικὴ Δημιουργία 12 (1953) 97–107.

MANOUSSAKAS (1955)
M. Manoussakas, 'La littérature crétoise à l'époque vénitienne', *L'Hellénisme contemporain* 9 (1955) 95–120.

MAVROCHALYVIDIS AND KESISOGLOU (1960)
G. Mavrochalyvidis and I. Kesisoglou, *Τὸ γλωσσικὸ ἰδίωμα τῆς Ἀξοῦ*, Athens, 1960.

MEGAS (1925)
A. Megas, *Ἱστορία τοῦ γλωσσικοῦ ζητήματος*, Athens, 1925.

MEILLET (1935)
A. Meillet, *Aperçu d'une histoire de la langue grecque*, 4th ed., Paris, 1935.

MEYER-LÜBKE (1889)
W. Meyer-Lübke, *Grammatica linguae Graecae vulgaris. Reproduction de l'édition de 1638, suivie d'un commentaire grammatical et historique*, Paris, 1889.

MIHĂESCU (1960)
H. Mihăescu, *Limba latină în provinciile dunărene de imperiului roman*, Bucharest, 1960.

MIHEVC (1959)
E. Mihevc, 'La disparition du parfait dans le grec de la basse époque', *Slovenska Akademja Znanosti in Umetnosti, Razred za filološke in literarne vede*, Razprave 5 (1959) 91–154.

MIHEVC-GABROVEC (1960)
E. Mihevc-Gabrovec, *Études sur la syntaxe de Ioannes Moschos*, Ljubljana, 1960.

MIRAMBEL (1929)
A. Mirambel, *Étude descriptive du parler maniote méridional*, Paris, 1929.

MIRAMBEL (1937)
A. Mirambel, *Les états de langue dans la Grèce actuelle* (Conférences de l'Institut de Linguistique de l'Université de Paris 5), Paris, 1937.

MIRAMBEL (1951)
A. Mirambel, 'Le roman néo-grec et la langue littéraire en Grèce', *Bulletin de l'Association Guillaume Budé*, 3ᵉ série, 1 (1951) 60–73.

MIRAMBEL (1953)
A. Mirambel, 'Les tendances actuelles de la dialectologie néo-hellénique', *Orbis* 2 (1953) 448–472.

MIRAMBEL (1955)
A. Mirambel, 'Morphologie et rôle fonctionnel de l'article dans les parlers néo-helléniques', *Bulletin de la Société de Linguistique* 51 (1955), 57–79.

MIRAMBEL (1957)
A. Mirambel, 'La doctrine linguistique de Jean Psichari', *La Nouvelle Clio* 3 (1957), 78–104.

MIRAMBEL (1957-8)
A. Mirambel, 'Genre et nombre dans la flexion des noms en grec moderne', *Bulletin de la Société de Linguistique* 53 (1957–8), 103–137.

MIRAMBEL (1959)
A. Mirambel, *La langue grecque moderne. Description et analyse*, Paris, 1959.

MIRAMBEL (1961)[1]
A. Mirambel, 'Participe et gérondif en grec médiéval et moderne', *Bulletin de la Société de Linguistique* 56 (1961) 46–79.

MIRAMBEL (1961)[2]
A. Mirambel, 'Le grec moderne', in *L'adaptation des langues 'classiques' aux besoins modernes dans le proche-orient (arabe, turc, persan, hébreu et grec modernes)*, Entretiens organisés les 25–27 avril 1961, Institut d'Études Islamiques et Centre d'Études de l'Orient contemporain de l'Université de Paris (Hors commerce, u.d.) xxi–xxiv, 77–100.

MIRAMBEL (1963)[1]
A. Mirambel, 'Pour une grammaire historique du grec médiéval', *Actes du XIIᵉ Congrès International des Études Byzantines*, Belgrade, 1963, II, 391–403.

MIRAMBEL (1963)[2]
A. Mirambel, 'Dialectes néo-Helléniques et syntaxe', *Bulletin de la Société de Linguistique* 58 (1963) 85–134.

MIRAMBEL (1964)[1]
A. Mirambel, 'Systèmes verbaux en grec moderne', *Bulletin de la Société de Linguistique* 59 (1964) 40–76.

MIRAMBEL (1964)[2]
A. Mirambel, 'Les aspects psychologiques du purisme dans la Grèce moderne', *Journal de Psychologie* (1964) 405–436.

MIRAMBEL (1965)
A. Mirambel, 'Remarques sur les systèmes vocaliques des dialectes néo-grecs d'Asie-Mineure', *Bulletin de la Société de Linguistique* 60 (1965) 18–45.

MIRAMBEL (1966)
A. Mirambel, 'Essai sur l'évolution du verbe en grec byzantin', *Bulletin de la Société de Linguistique* 61 (1968).

MORGAN (1960)
G. Morgan, *Cretan Poetry: sources and inspiration*, Heraklion, 1960.

MOULTON (1908)
J. H. Moulton, *A Grammar of N.T. Greek* (vol. I, *Prolegomena*), 3rd ed., Edinburgh, 1908.

NARAIN (1957)
A. K. Narain, *The Indo-Greeks*, Oxford, 1957.

OECONOMIDIS (1908)
D. E. Oeconomidis, *Lautlehre des Pontischen*, Leipzig, 1908.

PALMER (1934)
L. R. Palmer, 'Prolegomena to a Grammar of the Post-Ptolemaic Papyri', *Journal of Theological Studies* (1934), 170 ff.

PALMER (1939)
L. R. Palmer, 'Some Late Greek Ghost Words', *Classical Quarterly* 33 (1939) 31 ff.

PALMER (1945)
L. R. Palmer, *A Grammar of the Post-Ptolemaic Papyri* I, London, 1945.

PANKALOS (1955–60)
G. E. Pankalos, Περὶ τοῦ γλωσσικοῦ |ἰδιώματος τῆς Κρήτης, 4 vols, Athens, 1955–60.

PAPADOPOULOS (1926)
A. Papadopoulos, Γραμματικὴ τῶν Βορείων ἰδιωμάτων τῆς νέας Ἑλληνικῆς γλώσσης, Athens, 1926.

PAPADOPOULOS (1955)
A. Papadopoulos, Ἱστορικὴ γραμματικὴ τῆς Ποντικῆς διαλέκτου, Athens, 1955.

PAPADOPOULOS (1948)
I. Papadopoulos, Ἡ Κρήτη ὑπὸ τους Σαρακηνούς, Athens, 1948.

PARLANGELI (1953)
O. Parlangeli, 'Sui dialetti romanzi e romaici del Salento', *Memorie dell'Istituto Lombardo di Scienze e Lettere*, 25, fasc. 3, 1953.

PARLANGELI (1960)
O. Parlangeli, *Storia linguistica e storia politica dell'Italia meridionale*, Florence, 1960.

PERLES (1893)
J. Perles, 'Jüdisch-byzantinische Beziehungen', *Byzantinische Zeitschrift* 2 (1893) 569–584.

PERNOT (1891)
H. Pernot, 'L'indicatif présent du verbe être en néo-grec', *Mémoires de la Société de Linguistique* 9 (1891) 170–188.

PERNOT (1907)
H. Pernot, *Collection des monuments pour servir à l'étude de la langue néo-hellénique*, 3ᵉ série, 1, Paris, 1907.

PERNOT (1931)
H. Pernot, *Chansons populaires des XVᵉ et XVIᵉ siècles*, Paris, 1931.

PERNOT (1934)
H. Pernot, *Introduction à l'étude du dialecte tsakonien*, Paris, 1934.

PERNOT (1946)
H. Pernot, *Études de linguistique néo-hellénique II. Morphologie des parlers de Chio*, Paris, 1946.

PISANI (1947)
V. Pisani, *Manuale storico della lingua greca*, Florence, 1947.

POLITIS (1965–67)
L. Politis, Ποιητικὴ ἀνθολογία, Athens, 7 vols, 1965–67.

POP (1950)
S. Pop, *La dialectologie* II. Louvain 1950, 1047–1065.

PSALTES (1913)
G. B. Psaltes, *Grammatik der byzantinischen Chroniken*, Göttingen, 1913.

PSICHARI (1886–1889)
Psichari, *Essais de grammaire historique néo-grecque*, 2 vols, Paris, 1886–89.

RADERMACHER (1947)
L. Radermacher, *Koine, Sitzungsberichte der österreichischen Akademie der Wissenschaften*, 224, 5, Vienna, 1947.

REICHENKRON (1962)
G. Reichenkron, 'Der Typus der Balkansprachen', *Zeitschrift für Balkanologie* 1 (1962) 91–122.

ROHLFS (1924)
G. Rohlfs, *Griechen und Romanen in Unteritalien*, Munich, 1924.

ROHLFS (1930)
G. Rohlfs, *Etymologisches Wörterbuch der unteritalienischen Gräzität*, Halle, 1930.

ROHLFS (1933)
G. Rohlfs, *Scavi linguistici nella Magna Grecia*, Rome, 1933.

ROHLFS (1950)
G. Rohlfs, *Historische Grammatik der unteritalienischen Gräzität*, Munich, 1950.

ROHLFS (1962)
G. Rohlfs, *Neue Beiträge zur Kenntnis der unteritalienischen Gräzität*, Munich, 1962.

ROSETTI (1943)
A. Rosetti, *Istoria limbii romîne* I, 2nd ed., Bucharest, 1943.

ROSSI TAIBBI AND CARACAUSI (1959)
G. Rossi Taibbi and G. Caracausi, *Testi neogreci di Calabria*, Palermo, 1959.

RYDBECK (1967)
L. Rydbeck, *Fachprosa, vermeintliche Volkssprache und Neues Testament*, Uppsala, 1967.

SANDFELD (1930)
Kr. Sandfeld, *Linguistique balkanique. Problèmes et résultats*, Paris, 1930.

SCHMID (1887–97)
W. Schmid, *Der Attizismus in seinen Hauptvertretern von Dionysius von Halikarnassos bis auf den zweiten Philostratus*, 4 vols, Stuttgart, 1887–97.

SCHWYZER (1939)
E. Schwyzer, *Griechische Grammatik*, I, Munich, 1939, 45–137.

SEAMAN (1965)
P. D. Seaman, *Modern Greek and American English in contact: a socio-linguistic investigation of Greek American bilingualism in Chicago*, University of Indiana, Ph.D. Thesis, 1965 (microfilm).

SEILER (1952)
H.-J. Seiler, *L'aspect et le temps dans le verbe néo-grec*, Paris, 1952.

SEILER (1958)[1]
H.-J. Seiler, 'Zur Systematik und Entwicklungsgeschichte der griechischen Nominaldeklination', *Glotta* 37 (1958) 4–67.

SEILER (1958)[2]
H. J. Seiler, 'Das Problem der sogenannten Geminaten in den neugriechischen Dialekten mit besonderer Berücksichtigung einiger Dodekanes-Dialekte', *Glotta* 36 (1958) 209 ff.

SEMENOV (1935)
A. Semenov, 'Der nordpontische Dialekt des Neugriechischen', *Glotta* 23 (1935) 96 ff.

SERGIEVSKIJ (1934)
M. V. Sergievskij, Мариюпольские греческие говоры, Известия Академии Наук СССР. Отделение общественных Наук, 1934, 533–587.

SIAPKARAS-PITSILLIDES (1952)
Th. Siapkaras-Pitsillides, *Le Pétrarquisme en Chypre. Poèmes d'amour en dialecte chypriote d'après un manuscrit du XV*e *siècle*, Athens, 1952.

STARR (1962)
Chester G. Starr, *The Origins of Greek Civilisation*, London, 1962.

TABACHOVITZ (1943)
D. Tabachovitz, *Études sur le grec de la basse époque*, Uppsala, 1943.

TABACHOVITZ (1956)
D. Tabachovitz, *Die Septuaginta und das N.T.*, Lund, 1956.

TARN (1938)
W. W. Tarn, *The Greeks in Bactria and India*, Cambridge, 1938.

THOMSON (1960)
G. Thomson, *The Greek Language*, Cambridge, 1960.

THOMSON (1964)
G. Thomson, *Ἡ Ἑλληνικὴ γλῶσσα, ἀρχαία καὶ νέα*, Athens, 1964.

THUMB (1895)
A. Thumb, *Handbuch der neugriechischen Volkssprache*, Strassburg, 1895.

THUMB (1901)
A. Thumb, *Die griechische Sprache im Zeitalter des Hellenismus*, Strassburg, 1901.

TILL (1961)
W. Till, *Koptische Dialektgrammatik*, Munich, 1961.

TRAPP (1965)
E. Trapp, 'Der Dativ und der Ersatz seiner Funktion in der byzantinischen Vulgärdichtung bis zur Mitte des 15. Jahrhunderts', *Jahrbuch der österreichischen Byzantinischen Gesellschaft* 14 (1965) 21-34.

TRIANTAPHYLLIDES (1909)
M. Triantaphyllides, *Die Lehnwörter der mittelgriechischen Vulgärliteratur*, Strassburg, 1909 (reprinted in M. Triantaphyllides, *Ἅπαντα* I, Thessalonika, 1963).

TRIANTAPHYLLIDES (1937)
M. Triantaphyllides, *Σταθμοὶ τῆς γλωσσικῆς μας ἱστορίας*, Athens, 1937 (reprinted in M. Triantaphyllides, *Ἅπαντα* 5, Thessalonika, 1963, 308-365).

TRIANTAPHYLLIDES (1938)
M. A. Triantaphyllides, *Νεοελληνικὴ Γραμματική* I, Athens, 1938.

TRIANTAPHYLLIDES (1949)
M. Triantaphyllides, 'L'état présent de la question linguistique en Grèce', *Byzantion* 19 (1949) 281-288.

TRUBETZKOY (1939)
N. S. Trubetzkoy, *Grundzüge der Phonologie*, Prague, 1939.

TRYPANIS (1960)
C. A. Trypanis, 'Early Medieval Greek ἵνα', *Glotta* 38 (1960) 312-313.

VAN DIJK-WITTOP KONING (1963)
A. M. van Dijk-Wittop Koning, *De continuiteit van het Grieks. Onderzoek naar de herkomst van de woordvoorraad van het Nieuwgrieks*, Zwolle, 1963.

VASMER (1900)
M. Vasmer, Греко-славянские этюды, Известия ОРЯС 11 (1900)

VASMER (1907)
M. Vasmer, Греческие заимствования в русском языке, Известия ОРЯС 12 (1907)

VASMER (1909)
M. Vasmer, Греческие заимствования в русском языке, Сборник ОРЯС 6 (1909)

VASMER (1923)
M. Vasmer, *Ein russisch-byzantinisches Gesprächbuch*, Leipzig, 1923.

VERMEULE (1964)
E. T. Vermeule, *Greece in the Bronze Age*, Chicago, 1964.

VISCIDI (1944)
F. Viscidi, *I prestiti latini nel greco antico e bizantino*, Padua, 1944.

WAHRMANN (1907)
P. Wahrmann, *Prolegomena zu einer Geschichte der griechischen Dialekte im Zeitalter des Hellenismus*, Vienna, 1907.

WEIERHOLT (1963)
K. Weierholt, *Studien im Sprachgebrauch des Malalas*, Oslo, 1963.

WOLFF (1961)
H. J. Wolff, 'Der byzantinische Urkundenstil Ägyptens im Lichte der Funde von Nessana und Dura', *Revue internationale des droits de l'antiquité*, 3ᵉ série, 8 (1961) 115–154.

WOODCOCK (1966)
G. Woodcock, *The Greeks in India*, London, 1966.

WORRELL (1934)
W. H. Worrell, *Coptic Sounds*, Ann Arbor, 1934.

XANTHOUDIDES (1915)
S. A. Xanthoudides, 'Ερωτόκριτος. "Εκδοσις κριτική. Heraklion, 1915.

ZILLIACUS (1935)
H. Zilliacus, *Zum Kampf der Weltsprachen im spätrömischen Reich*, Helsinki, 1935.

ZILLIACUS (1967)
H. Zilliacus, *Zur Abundanz der spätgriechischen Gebrauchssprache*, Helsinki, 1967.

GLOSSARY

Affricate
A consonant beginning as a plosive but ending as a spirant, e.g. English *ch*.

Aspect
A verbal category indicating the way in which the action of the verb is envisaged by the speaker, e.g. as continuous, instantaneous, habitual, etc. The differences between 'I go' and 'I am going', or between 'sit' and 'sit down', are differences of aspect.

Athematic
In an athematic verb in Greek the personal endings are attached directly to the verb stem.

Calque
A word or expression whose meaning, and sometimes whose form, is modelled upon that of a word in another language to which it is felt to be an equivalent. Thus English 'epoch-making' is not a natural English formation, but a calque of German 'epochemachend'.

Consecutive
A consecutive clause expresses the out-come or result of the action of the main clause.

Demotic
The living, spoken form of Modern Greek, now also used for most literary purposes.

Denominative

A denominative verb is formed from a noun, e.g. βασιλεύω 'I reign' from βασιλεύς 'king'.

Diglossy

The habitual use by a community of two clearly distinguished forms of the same language in different situations. The child who speaks York-shire dialect at home but the Queen's English at school is practising diglossy.

Dvandra

A copulative compound, the two elements of which are merely com-bined, neither determining the other. Modern Greek μαχαιροπέρουνο 'knife and fork, couvert' is a dvandra compound. English 'knife-grinder' is a determinative compound.

Final

A final clause expresses the purpose or aim of the action of the main clause.

Imparisyllabic

Having a special plural suffix, so that plural forms contain one more syllable than singular, e.g. Modern Greek παπᾶς—παπᾶδει.

Katharevousa

The learned, archaising form of Modern Greek.

Klephtic

The Klephtic ballads celebrated the exploits of the bands of Greeks who took to the mountains rather than submit to Turkish domination. The word Klepht (κλέφτης) originally means 'robber'.

Koine

The common Greek of the Hellenistic world, basically Attic, but distinct from all local dialects.

Neo-Grammarians

A school of linguists in the late nineteenth century, who insisted on the discovery of rigid laws of phonetic change between different stages of a language, or between two related languages.

Optative

A mood of the Ancient Greek verb used to express wish and potentiality, distinct in form from indicative, subjunctive and imperative.

Parisyllabic

Having the same number of syllables in its plural form as in its singular, e.g. Modern Greek ναύτης—ναῦτει.

Periphrastic

A periphrastic verbal form employs a secondary verb in its formation. 'I was going', 'I would go' are periphrastic; 'I go', 'I went' are not.

Phonology

The structure of systematic distinctions of sounds made by the speakers of a language, excluding individual variations in pronunciation, local or class accents, etc.

Plosive

A consonant in the pronunciation of which the flow of the breath is interrupted. *P* and *b* are plosives, *l* and *m* are not.

Polyseury

The use of the same word with a number of different meanings. Thus 'operation' means something different in a military context from what it means in a medical context.

Spirant

A consonant in the pronunciation of which the stream of breath is forced through a narrow opening in the vocal apparatus, but not interrupted e.g. *f*, *v*, *s*.

Synizesis

The pronunciation of two originally distinct but contiguous vowels in a single syllable. The final syllable of modern English 'nation' is a result of the synizesis of the earlier *-ti-on*.

Theme

The form of a verb stem to which personal endings are attached. A verb in Greek may have different themes in different tenses.

Thematic

In a thematic verb in Greek the personal endings are not attached directly to the verb stem, but are preceded by a vowel.

INDEX